THE FINANCIAL
CORNERSTONE

THE FINANCIAL CORNERSTONE

Following the Biblical Roadmap for Finances

PHILIP BROWN

Trilogy Christian Publishers A Wholly Owned Subsidiary of Trinity Broadcasting Network
2442 Michelle Drive Tustin, CA 92780

Manufactured in the United States of America

10 9 8 7 6 5 4 3 2 1

Library of Congress Cataloging-in-Publication Data is available.

ISBN: 978-1-64088-475-5

E-ISBN: 978-1-64088-476-2

ACKNOWLEDGEMENTS

Since this is my first published book there are many people I must thank for their contributions over the years. First, I would like to thank my parents Audrey and Lyle Brown who tolerated my reading habits and created an environment which encouraged independent thinking and personal expression. Next is my brother Nat and sister Naomi who have always been there no matter what life has sent my way.

I want to thank Sharon Halter for encouraging me to enter writing contests in Junior High, which led to a summer writing workshop at Laramie County Community College. With High School came Peter Holcomb who, although he was not a spiritual man, was deeply religious about searching for the truth and writing clearly without being verbose. Thrown in the mix was Randy Larson who taught the basics of real journalism and digging for facts.

I must thank my wife Becky and daughter Emily for giving me the time and space to finish writing this book. I also must thank her father Charles for teaching me to play chess at an early age and getting me interested in theology.

I want to thank Trinity Publishing for their expert advice and skills with getting this book published. I thank Laura McElroy and Joe Wilken for content suggestions. I also appreciate a small group of friends and family who helped make this book a reality.

TABLE OF CONTENTS

INTRODUCTION

There are three basic categories of financial books: investing, general money management, and managing money from a religious viewpoint. There are thousands of books in each category, many of them repeating the same general advice from a slightly different perspective. With so many options available, why would anyone bother to write another one?

One reason books keep coming out is financial products are being introduced at an incredible rate. While they might sound new and exciting, they are typically recycled concepts packaged under new names with flashy new logos. It may pay better to write new books and present the concepts as original ideas, but it would be more useful for a popular financial magazine to come out with a yearly article listing the "new" products and what old concepts and products they were derived from.

The one category of books that are exempt from this problem are the religious-oriented books, especially from a Christian standpoint. They have an even bigger problem: all the concepts are very old and do not change. Because of this, recent books tend to rush over the religious concepts to focus on the latest products. The Christian concepts are still there but are often breezed over so quickly their importance is lost.

While this book does introduce some "new" concepts that are really decades old, the purpose is to refocus on the Christian fundamentals. While products and techniques are important, it is my belief they are ultimately worthless if they are not used from the proper perspective. Using the best financial techniques without a proper Christian relationship is like going to church for purely business reasons: there might be temporary advantages, but ultimately your motives will come out, and the results typically are not what you are hoping.

I did the research for this book twice. The first time I was blindly searching for verses related to money, and the list is long. After getting distracted for a few years, I picked up this project again—only to discover that in process of changing computers three or four times and going from floppy discs to CDs to thumb drives, I couldn't open the old files. This launched several more months of re-compiling the list with a different perspective. Instead of just throwing the verses into categories, I began seeing some general themes come out.

Some of the themes have become bastardized by American culture and are now demonized, even though they are engrained in the Bible. Some have been blown out of proportion by the sects who originally colonized the United States and tend to overshadow the well-balanced approach represented by the Bible as a whole. In general, the materialistic culture that has overtaken the United States overshadows what is important, which is using all your gifts of time, money, and possessions to support your family and the less fortunate.

In the interest of making the information in this book understandable to the largest audience, all references are from the New International Version of the Bible.

START WITH THE SOURCE

There are so many financial topics in the Bible that deciding which one to start with seemed overwhelming at first. My second round of research made it obvious, however. Many people are so busy getting "stuff" they forget where the "stuff" comes from. It reminds me of the part of the scientific community who focus on the minute details of what they know, when most of their focus turns out to be the outside products of complex chains of reactions that takes decades to uncover. We can only find balance in our financial lives by digging far beyond the details and focusing on the essence.

It seems trite to say God is the source of everything. He created everything, so of course he is the source. If we can see something with our imperfect vision, even if it is light years away sensed at the end of the most complex technology we have invented, it came from God. All of our most wild, imperfect theories with a hint of supporting information are poor attempts to describe the complex world we live in.

Despite the complexity of the world around us, all too often we are content to grab whatever object is in front of us, seize it, and be content to call it "mine." While we may officially control it, we forget both the object and our bodies are only temporary. Most of the "stuff" we care so much about will be broken and forgotten within five years, and even our bodies will return to dirt in a few years. The atoms and molecules our stuff and bodies now contain will soon be recycled into dirt and grass, no matter how many chemicals are pumped into our corpse. The source remains, the created bits and pieces still in use, but the items and forms we are so proud of will be dim memories at best.

It is good to be reminded of all the different things God created we take advantage of every day. The further away from nature we drive ourselves, the harder it is to remember the simple parts of creation we should be thankful for. If we only recognize and appreciate the complex, we lose contact with the basics necessary for life. The drive for what is new and innovative blocks our appreciation of what is important, creating a vicious cycle pulling us away from appreciating the fundamentals of life.

The more technology advances, the faster we think we need things, and the more we settle for low quality. We must have food fast to fit into our lifestyle, so we settle for a low quality burger instead of taking the time to buy and make a home-made meal even though the increased calories and added preservatives mean a shorter lifespan dependent on drugs to improve our quality of life. We willingly pay thousands of dollars more for a car that looks different or drives faster while ignoring the increased maintenance costs and short expected lifespan. We pay thousands more for a house in a "desirable" neighborhood based on location or schools without considering the poor quality of construction, higher taxes and transportation costs, and increased pollution in the area. These move us farther from the source of a quality lifestyle and the importance of health, family, and a religious foundation.

Here is a short list of the truly important things in life, and how God is the ultimate source of each. We grow food from plants God created in land God made using water God created in order to survive. God created people and a way to reproduce, so he is responsible for the families who provide us food, shelter, and an environment to learn how to care for ourselves and a work ethic to provide for ourselves as we mature. God provided us the physical and mental capabilities to not only earn a living, but also to carefully plan and strategize using what we earn to provide for ourselves both now and in the future. God created the senses we use to understand what is going on around us and the emotions responding to those situations so we can enjoy our families and activities. When we constantly focus on the Now and instant gratification, we not only lose our understanding of what is important but also appreciation for the source of all the things we need and have.

Land: Psalms 24:1-2, Psalms 104:10-18, Acts 14:14-17

Water: Job 36:27-33, Psalms 65:9-13, Psalms 107:33-38

Food: Psalms 67:6-7, Psalms 85:12, Isaiah 30:23-26

Enjoyment:	Proverbs 3, Proverbs 28:26, Ecclesiastes 2:24-26
Family:	Psalms 68:5-6, Psalms 68:9-10, Psalms 146:6-9
Wealth:	Genesis 14:22-24, Job 22:21-25, Isaiah 45:5-7

Losing sight of the source of life and wealth causes many issues. The largest one can be found in 1 Timothy 6:10 "For the love of money is a root of all kinds of evil. Some people, eager for money, have wandered from the faith and pierced themselves with many griefs." Focusing on the transient currency we use to get the temporary things we think we need to survive throws opens the door to using unethical and sometime illegal methods to get what we want.

One shortcut we use to get what we want is bribery and extortion. Bribery is using resources to unjustly influence someone in a responsible position to skew a decision in someone's favor. Extortion is when the person in a responsible position demands a payment before making a decision. There were two common methods of bribery in Bible times. The first was through financial means, as shown in Deuteronomy 10:7, "For the Lord your God is God of gods and Lord of lords, the great God, mighty and awesome, who shows no partiality and accepts no bribes," and Proverbs 17:8, "A bribe is seen as a charm by the one who gives it; they think success will come at every turn." In the New Testament after Jesus rose the Pharisees bribed the guards to claim his body was stolen in Matthew 28:12-15, "When the chief priests had met with the elders and devised a plan, they gave the soldiers a large sum of money, telling them, "You are to say, 'His disciples came during the night and stole him away while we were asleep.' If this report gets to the governor, we will satisfy him and keep you out of trouble." So the soldiers took the money and did as they were instructed. And this story has been widely circulated among the Jews to this very day." Bribery and extortion often go hand in hand as we find in Ezekiel 22:12 which says, "'In you are people who accept bribes to shed blood; you take interest and make a profit from the poor. You extort unjust gain from your neighbors. And you have forgotten me,' declares the Sovereign Lord." In either bribery or extortion, a person in authority biases their decision on an issue based on a financial payment or other consideration.

Now we use other ways to bribe those around us, probably used proficiently in ancient times but not specifically mentioned in the Bible. Sex is frequently used to influence decisions, both explicitly and by dressing certain ways and flirting with those in authority. Political influence is another common way of influencing issues in someone's favor. Even the simple act of performing chores for someone can be misused as bribery, from something as simple as mowing the lawn to the insidious such as murdering someone for someone else. The most evil way people use bribes is emotionally through superficial love or sex to persuade people to do what they want without any serious emotional attachment. While many of the favors people do for others are done with good intentions, when we leverage them to obtain the outcomes we desire, they rise to the level of a bribe.

A similar perversion of influence is found in the misuse of gifts. Gifts are commonly used to show appreciation for someone else, typically used at holidays, between married and dating couples, or from individuals or companies to show appreciation. They can just as easily be misused to obtain influence in ways as varied as inappropriate gifts between employee and employer, supplier and company, and lobbyist and politician. Some verses you can find the misuse of gifts include Isaiah 1:23, Micah 7:3, 1 Kings 13:7-10 and Micah 1:7. Real gifts are designed to show appreciation, either for a person or something they have accomplished. Sometimes gifts are given because of who a person is, such as Christmas gifts for relatives or hostess gifts for dinner invitations. In every instance, the gift is a physical way to show appreciation for something but can be used inappropriately.

Another way we try to bypass acknowledging the source of our existence is through deception or cheating. Deception is presenting something for a different value than it is. Common ways we see this are car salesmen giving more in trade in value for cars after inflating the cost of their inventory and companies raising the cost of certain items just before putting them "on sale" for the original price. Other modern ways we typically practice this is by overstating qualifications on resumes, spray painting rust spots before selling used cars, pretending to be a different person while dating and putting on a false front to cover personal and marital issues. The first example of cheating we find in the Bible is found in Genesis 31:1-16 where Jacob placed sticks in front of watering holes to cause Labin's ewes to have spotted lambs instead of pure white ones. Unjust transactions were warned against in Proverbs 11:1, "The Lord detests dishonest scales, but accurate weights find favor with him," and Haggai 2:16, "When anyone came to a heap of twenty measures, there were only ten. When anyone went to a wine vat to draw fifty measures, there were only twenty." Deception is not a sales technique: it is a character flaw that repeats itself in all aspects of life.

Coveting what other people have is a way to deny the source of our being. Close relatives of coveting are envy and jealousy. While it is fine, and even healthy, to admire what other people have and strive to obtain things for ourselves, coveting is a cancer of envying what others have and ignoring the responsibility we have to earn posessions or spouses for ourselves. Coveting at its root is blaming others for earning more or more wisely managing their money and actions instead of taking responsibility to learn how to earn more or act more appropriately to get what we desire with our own efforts. It is a part of the Ten Commandments in Deuteronomy 5:21, which says "You shall not covet your neighbor's wife. You shall not set your desire on your neighbor's house or land, his male or female servant, his ox or donkey, or anything that belongs to your neighbor." It is spelled out in Proverbs 12:12, "The wicked desire the stronghold of evildoers, but the root of the righteous endures." James 4:2-3 expands it more by saying "You desire but do not have, so you kill. You covet but you cannot get what you want, so you quarrel and fight. You do not have because you do not ask God. When you ask, you do not receive, because you ask with wrong motives, that you may spend what you get on your pleasures." God is the source of all things, so if we desire more we must ask God for it. God will answer the request with either yes if we have developed the knowledge and skills to handle it, or no if we are not yet prepared for it.

Pride is a fatal side effect when we attempt to claim responsibility for what we have instead of acknowledging God as the source. As Proverbs 16:18 puts it, "Pride goes before destruction, a haughty spirit before a fall." King Saul lost his kingdom to David because he decided rituals were more important than waiting on God's timing. Judas Iscariot's desire for wealth led to suicide after he betrayed Jesus for thirty pieces of silver. There are examples all around us where people have prioritized wealth over family and reputation which resulted in financial ruin. Without God we would not exist, and God gives us everything we have, so someone taking pride in what "they" have accomplished is arrogant at best. We should be satisfied by things we accomplish using our talents and abilities but taking pride in the accomplishment leads us away from the source. Recognition should come from others, which gives an ego check to how much importance we place on what we do. Instead of spending our time telling others how great the things are we have done, we should spend our time recognizing the little things others have done and allowing others to recognize the valuable things we do.

If keeping focused on the source is so important, finding ways to maintain that focus should be a constant part of life. Here is a list of ways to monitor where your focus is to make sure it isn't starting to waver:

1. What do you focus on the first thing in the morning and when you close your eyes at night?

2. What do you think about the most?

3. What do you talk about the most?

4. What do you spend the most money on after your bills are paid?

5. What do you doodle about?

6. What do you dream about, both asleep and awake?

7. What would your close friends and family say is most important to you?

Dreams and goals are a vital part of a healthy psyche. Without them life becomes a meaningless rut we mentally die in, no matter what age we are when it happens. Spending hours planning on how to achieve those goals is also important for mental health and making those dreams become realities. They become dangerous when we become consumed with those goals and visions to the extent of losing sight of who they come from and who gives us the abilities to achieve them. The next danger level is putting the achievement of them above caring physically and emotionally for our families and those around us.

Some might think that focusing on the source is dangerous as well. The fear of becoming a religious zealot by seeing everything coming from God and depending on the Holy Spirit to understand how to best utilize our gifts and abilities is unfounded because God's focus is on our best welfare and caring for others as Matthew 22:33-40 states; "Hearing that Jesus had silenced the Sadducees, the Pharisees got together. One of them, an expert in the law, tested him with this question: 'Teacher, which is the greatest commandment in the Law?' Jesus replied: "'Love the Lord your God with all your heart and with all your soul and with all your mind.'" This is the first and greatest commandment. And the second is like it: "'Love your neighbor as yourself.'" All the Law and the Prophets hang on these two commandments.'" Focusing on becoming more like God means we demonstrate the values and characteristics in the Love Chapter of 1 Corinthians 13. In fact, by becoming more like Christ we will achieve our goals in ways that are admired and appreciated instead of despised and feared. Focusing on the source brings more success and prosperity than trying to do it on our own.

FAMILY SECOND

The idea family should be designated as the second priority in your life may upset you for two reasons. One group of people will tell you their family is everything, which is wrong for Christians because God (the Source) must come first in your life. The second group of people will tell you it is most important to be happy and take care of yourself, which is also not scriptural because following God's priorities makes life run much smoother than trying to put yourself first, which is the definition of selfishness.

If we start talking about priorities, then we of course need a list. Here is a list of Christian priorities in the order most theologians and psychologists place it. Since I am a self-taught theologian and find many of current psychology's behavioral theories highly questionable, I'm sure you will disagree with it one way or the other, but since God did not make a list for us in the Bible, I am fine if you shift any below the first two.

1. God – always put the Source first

2. Family – those who you are responsible for and have taken care of you

    a. Spouse – giving anyone a higher priority than your spouse is fatal to any marriage

    b. Children – care for them until they are adults, including training them to be adults

    c. Parents – care for them when it becomes necessary for as long as you are able

    d. Extended – in extreme emergencies help them

3. Occupation – earn a living so you can provide for yourself and your family

4. Community – take responsibility for those around you

5. Country – it is important to support your government, even when you disagree with it

6. Hobbies – mental and physical distractions are healthy but the other priorities must be met first

Some priority lists separate the types of family, but this somewhat clouds the issue. By placing all of your family divisions together, it is easier to see that not all family should be given the same priority. It is important to talk about the strength of commitment you should make to each family type, both in length of time and how much responsibility you should assume for them.

At the top of the family priority list is your spouse if you have one. Your commitment to your spouse should be complete. Genesis 2:24 sums it up when it says, "That is why a man leaves his father and mother and is united to his wife, and they become one flesh." Ephesians 5:31 quotes this verse when it discussed the priority of family in the life of a Christian. When you are married, you should not do anything without involving your spouse, as if they were physically attached to you. Although this is not a book on marriage, it is key to having a successful marriage and vital to successfully managing a family's finances.

It is a good idea for each one of you to have some money to spend on every day needs and hobbies, but how much should be a joint decision. Budgeting is critical to anyone seeking financial success, but even more so with families. The first step in budgeting is determining how much money is committed to paying bills every month, and when those bills are due. After the bills are covered, the rest should be divided between planning for the future (savings and investments), covering daily needs (food, utilities and transportation) and personal care (clothes, haircuts and hobbies). Since this book is not focused on financial plans or techniques, I will not go into the details of how to make a budget, but there are thousands of books and other resources available to aid you in creating one.

Children are the second family priority. Proverbs 13:22 emphasizes this when it says, "A good person leaves an inheritance for their children's children, but a sinner's wealth is stored up for the righteous." 1 Thessalonians 2:11-12 emphasizes the training aspect of parenting with, "For you know that we dealt with each of you as a father deals with his own children, encouraging, comforting, and urging you to live lives worthy of God, who calls you into his kingdom and glory." Joshua is essentially the story of Israel returning to the Promised Land and conquering the lands God gave them, which he divided based on tribes and families. The value of a work ethic in children is mentioned in Proverbs 10:4-5 which says, "Lazy hands make for poverty, but diligent hands bring wealth. He who gathers crops in summer is a prudent son, but he who sleeps during harvest is a disgraceful son." A parent's responsibility to provide for and train their children is woven throughout the Bible.

If you have children in your house, they should be treated equally. If stepchildren are involved, it is vital that you and your spouse decide the financial approach for them and ensure children and stepchildren are treated the same. The ultimate goal in raising children from a financial standpoint is to teach them how to handle money responsibly so they are prepared to care for themselves and a family as soon as they leave the house as adults. For a Christian, this includes tithing, giving, budgeting, planning for the future, and spending less than they earn. Since children learn the basics of financial management from their parents by age seven, it is critical for parents to learn how to plan and manage money before they have children.

Children is where the first family priority caveat comes into play. If you raise them appropriately, your children will know how to manage money well when they leave the house as adults. If you raised them right, they will also have a work ethic where they understand they are responsible to earn a living and provide for themselves. Parents do a grave disservice to their children when they allow their children to depend on them for financial support after they become adults, as this delays their maturity and does not prepare them to care for their own families when they come. There are times when children first move out that financial crisis may occur and helping them out in these rare instances are fine, but it should not be a consistent pattern caused by poor financial management. A way to guarantee conflict in a family, both in life and after parents die, is for them to constantly give money to one child because they continually mismanage money and not give equal treatment to the other children.

Another issue with children is the concept of allowance. First and foremost, an allowance is not a bribe to get to do them to do chores. Adults do not get paid to do chores, and it is wrong to teach children they deserve to be paid to do the essential tasks of living. An allowance is a tool to teach children how to manage money correctly. Paying children for doing things above and beyond their chores is fine, but the money they earn and gifts they receive should all be combined and treated the same when teaching them financial habits. For example, children should pay tithe from their own money. They should be required to set aside at least ten percent in a long-term savings or money market account to pay for their own car and college expenses when the time comes. Making children pay for their own special clothes or wants is also important, as it teaches the value of planning ahead and combats the draws of materialism and instant gratification encouraged by parents paying allowance ahead or simply covering the difference on a consistent basis.

Parents are next in line for having financial priority in your life. Mark 7:10-13 states their importance when it says, "For Moses said, 'Honor your father and mother,' and, 'Anyone who curses their father or mother is to be put to death.' But you say that if anyone declares that what might have been used to help their father or mother is Corban (that is, devoted to God)—then you no longer let them do anything for their father or mother. Thus you nullify the word of God by your tradition that you have handed down. And you do many things like that." These verses establish the importance of caring for your parents and prioritizes their care above giving to the church or other causes. This is reiterated in 1 Timothy 5:3-4 which says, "Give proper recognition to those widows who are really in need. But if a widow has children or grandchildren, these should learn first of all to put their religion into practice by caring for their own family and so repaying their parents and grandparents, for this is pleasing to God." It is mentioned in 1 Timothy 5:8 as well, "Anyone who does not provide for their relatives, and especially for their own household, has denied the faith and is worse than an unbeliever."

Caring for your parents also comes with a caveat. They should live independently as long as possible to maintain their dignity and self-respect. However, when they become unable to adequately care for themselves, it is God's plan for the family to step up and provide the care they need. That may be as basic as covering the cost of installing a walk-in shower. It may be a long-term commitment, such as spending time with them every day to make sure they have healthy meals or splitting the cost of aide with the other siblings if you live too far away to care for them yourself. It may mean becoming their guardian if they become unable to make wise financial decisions themselves. Since caring for parents can be a large financial commitment, it should be an issue planned for years in advance to lessen the impact on your own family when the time comes.

Extended family should not be ignored in times of extreme financial hardship. The key to extreme financial hardship is it is rare, does not last an extended amount of time, and is not the result of consistent financial mismanagement on their part. It is their responsibility to adequately manage their own finances for day-to-day commitments and overspending on credit cards or vehicles or houses does not count as financial hardship someone else bails them out of. Proverbs 19:7 states this when it says, "The poor are shunned by all their relatives—how much more do their friends avoid them! Though the poor pursue them with pleading, they are nowhere to be found." Bad choices must be experiences they learn from as they mature, and other people enabling their bad choices gives them a free pass to make more bad choices if they continually shift the consequences onto others.

Cosigning loans for anyone other than your spouse must be avoided at all costs. No matter how much you care for your parents, children, or extended family, your financial responsibility lies primarily to your spouse. If the other person loses their job or decides they should spend their money on hobbies instead of bills, you are committed to covering the payments, which affects the financial condition of your spouse and children. If you can afford to assume that loan, it would be better for you to simply give them enough money to cover part of the cost and use that for a down payment to allow them to qualify for the loan on their own.

Although family must be the second priority in a Christian's life, relatives should be treated differently depending on how close they are to you. A spouse should be an equal partner when determining priorities and budgets. Children should be cared for while in the house but trained to correctly manage their own money from a very young age, so they can successfully care for themselves when they leave home. Parents should remain independent as long as possible, but the family should care for them when they can no longer do it themselves. Extended families should be provided assistance in emergency situations only. By maintaining the proper level of financial assistance to each level of your family, you provide care to those in need while protecting your own family's resources.

Figure 1

Biblical Financial Priority List

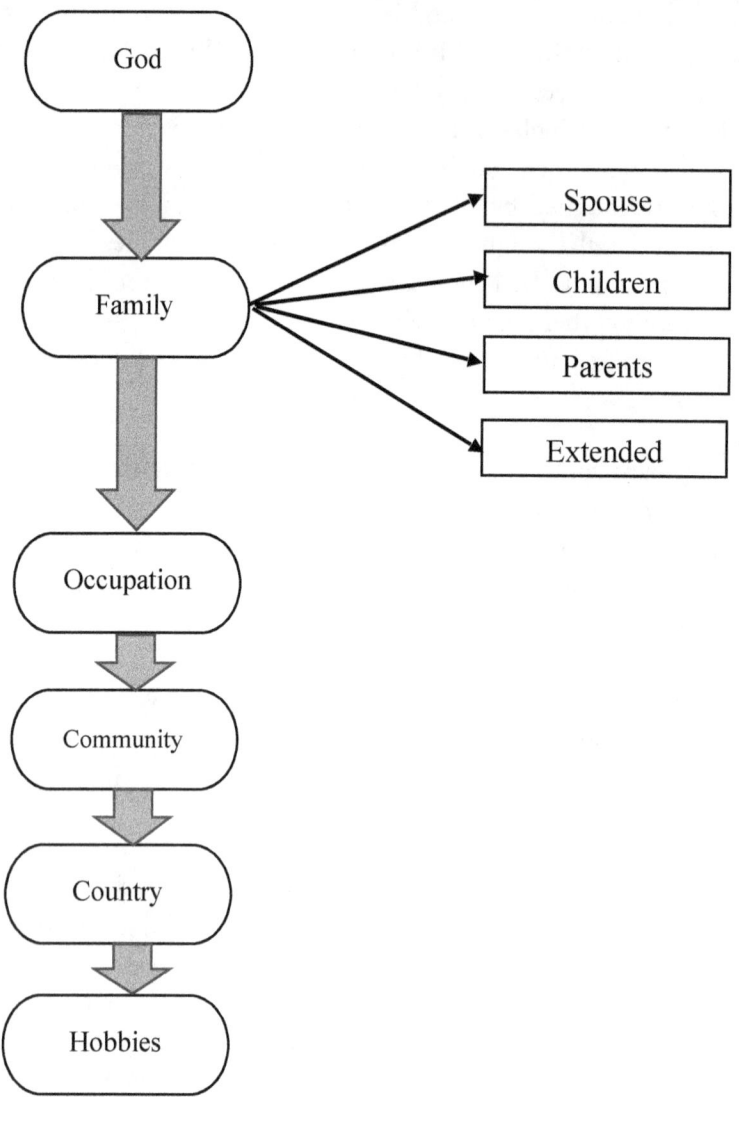

TITHES AND OFFERINGS

Tithing might be the most loathed sermon topic of all time. It does not matter which part of the world you go to, what language it is spoken in, or even which denomination the subject is raised, it causes a queasy feeling in part of the congregation. Everyone knows you are supposed to do it. Many feel they have a special situation that should partially or fully exempt them right now. No matter how much money you make, there is always something out there that part of your income could help with more than giving it to support a religious cause.

Except this isn't true. As Jentezen Franklin put it in a sermon, the pastor or leader talking about tithing isn't the problem. They are just the doctor performing a religious examination. If it hurts when they touch the subject of tithing, they are not the problem. The problem is your priorities and spending habits. If your focus is on God, and you recognize Him as the source of all your blessings, then giving a tenth back to Him is not an issue.

It also makes a difference with your location. Those who eke out an income of pennies a day, live in single room huts, and walk everywhere consistently give a larger part of their income to support their local church than those who live in large houses with all the modern amenities and own more than one car. This goes back to the cultural bias of technology driving people to focus more on themselves as they live farther away from the Source, daily visible in the dirt of the farm but hidden behind the screen of a computer.

Your income level also tends to skew your view of the Source as well. If you earn very little and are forced to watch your spending closely, you usually not only appreciate what you have more but also willingly tithe and are more generous to those around you. This is found in Mark 12:41-44 where Jesus pointed out a widow who gave everything she had to the temple offering and ignored the religious leaders who poured bags of pennies into the offering box after having someone literally blow a horn to get everyone's attention to their supposed generosity. In Matthew 6:3-4 Jesus said, "But when you give to the needy, do not let your left hand know what your right hand is doing, so that your giving may be in secret. Then your Father, who sees what is done in secret, will reward you." If you give your tithe, offerings, or gifts so other people will give you recognition for your generosity you may get temporary recognition from people but miss out on the blessings God describes in Malachi 3:10, "'Bring the whole tithe into the storehouse, that there may be food in my house. Test me in this,' says the Lord Almighty, 'and see if I will not throw open the floodgates of heaven and pour out so much blessing that there will not be room enough to store it.'"

Now that I have reminded you of why you should tithe, we should go over how to. Most people have often heard this but desperately try to finagle some way so it will "cost" them less. If the cost is still an issue, the issue is not tithing by priorities. Cost is only an issue if you are not tithing or do not tithe enough. The more you tithe with the right priorities and attitude the more you will understand the blessings you receive are far greater than the small thank you gift you return to God.

Tithing was initiated early in the Old Testament. It is first mentioned in Genesis 14:18-20 which says, "Then Melchizedek king of Salem brought out bread and wine. He was priest of the God Most High, and he blessed Abram, saying, 'Blessed be Abram by God Most High, Creator of heaven and earth. And praise be to God Most High, who delivered your enemies into your hand.' Then Abram gave him a tenth of everything." Although this was before the law was given, it contains the two main qualifications for tithing. First, it was given to the local priest so it is to the local church. Secondly, it was ten percent of everything he had looted. The third element of tithing is found in Ex 23:19 where it says, "Bring the best of the firstfruits of your soil to the house of the Lord your God." The tithe should be the first money that comes out of your pocket after you earn it, not something you do with what is left over after you pay the bills and have your fun for the month. Following all three guidelines mean you are paying your tithe the way God defines it.

Tithing is made an official part of the Old Testament law in Leviticus 27:30-33 which says, "A tithe of everything from the land, whether grain from the soil or fruit from the trees, belongs to the Lord; it is holy to the Lord. Whoever would redeem any of their tithe must add a fifth of the value to it. Every tithe of the herd and flock—every tenth animal that passes under the shepherd's rod—will be holy to the Lord. No one may pick out the good from the bad or make any substitution. If anyone does make a substitution, both the animal and its substitute become holy and cannot be redeemed." Not only does it say the first tenth should be given to the priests, it says if you decide part of your tithe animals or crops is something you want to keep you must add an additional fifth (twenty percent) to your total offering. This theme runs through the entire chapter and is a concept that has been neglected for many years, that if you hang on to what God commands you return to Him then it will cost you more the longer you hang onto it.

The command changed slightly when the Israelites reached the Promised Land, and the temple was built. God tells them in Leviticus 26:1-4, "When you have entered the land the Lord your God is giving you as an inheritance and have taken possession of it and settled in it, take some of the firstfruits of all that you produce from the soil of the land the Lord your God is giving you and put them in a basket. Then go to the place the Lord your God will choose as a dwelling for his Name and say to the priest in office at the time, 'I declare today to the Lord your God that I have come to the land the Lord swore to our ancestors to give us.' The priest shall take the basket from your hands and set it down in front of the altar of the Lord your God." Instead of giving the tithe to the local priest, they were commanded to gather it and take it to the temple in Jerusalem. The supplies then were stored in the outer rooms of the temple to feed the priests who rotated through for their terms of service.

The most famous blessing and curse about tithing isn't found until Malachi. After many years of following idols and letting the temple fall into disrepair, the temple was rebuilt, and the Israelites began to worship God again under Nehemiah. After returning from giving an update to King Artaxerxes, he found the people had once again started worshipping idols and not tithing to the temple. His response, found in Malachi 3:8-12 was, "'Will a mere mortal rob God? Yet you rob me. But you ask, "How are we robbing you?" In tithes and offerings. You are under a curse—your whole nation—because you are robbing me. Bring the whole tithe into the storehouse, that there may be food in my house. Test me in this,' says the Lord

Almighty, 'and see if I will not throw open the floodgates of heaven and pour out so much blessing that there will not be room enough to store it. I will prevent pests from devouring your crops, and the vines in your fields will not drop their fruit before it is ripe,' says the Lord Almighty. 'Then all the nations will call you blessed, for yours will be a delightful land,' says the Lord Almighty." God reminded the Israelites they were being punished partly for not paying their tithes, then challenged them to test Him by putting their trust in the Source to see what blessings He would give them for their obedience.

After the book of Malachi we come to Matthew. There are many in the modern first world church who claim God's design for giving changed with the transition from Old Testament law to New Testament relationship. Many define this as Christians should still give ten percent of their income to God, but it is ok to only give part of this to the local church and use the rest to support other religious causes and those in need. While the law-versus-relationship transition did change many aspects of how Christians experience and express their relationship with God, I do not find any evidence for this perspective in either what Jesus or the young church taught. What I do see is more of a focus on the motives of the giver, not how the giving is defined.

The attitude over action is emphasized in Matthew 23:23 and Luke 11:42, which are based on the same event. Matthew 23:23 says, "Woe to you, teachers of the law and Pharisees, you hypocrites! You give a tenth of your spices—mint, dill, and cumin. But you have neglected the more important matters of the law—justice, mercy, and faithfulness. You should have practiced the latter, without neglecting the former." The Pharisees were so focused on appearances they not only tithed their finances and crops, but also took a tenth of every herb harvested for their cooking and gave it to the temple. They also put on a show when they gave so everyone would see what a conscientious giver they were. While I'm sure the priests appreciated having some extra flavor in their food, Jesus viewed their tithe as something contemptible because it was all for show instead of gratefully crediting God for being the Source of their life.

Matthew 5:23-24 brings it back to attitude when it says, "Therefore, if you are offering your gift at the altar and there remember that your brother or sister has something against you, leave your gift there in front of the altar.

First go and be reconciled to them; then come and offer your gift." This emphasizes once again your relationship with God is not only mirrored by, but depends on, your relationship with others. Many people act as if they can buy God's favor through tithes and offerings to cover broken relationships they refuse to heal through forgiveness, but it does not work that way. God is simply not interested in your gifts at any level until you have humbled yourself and restored the relationships you have broken or know are broken towards you. He prefers to take the gifts of those who have done the hard work of restoration to fulfill His purposes and uses the opportunity to bless those who have given with the right attitudes along the way.

The question we must ask is, where did the idea of tithing no longer belonging to the local church come from? If it is only based on the idea of no longer being under the law, should the same concept be applied to the Ten Commandments as well? It is convenient to give our money to our favorite causes instead of the local church, and there is no question they go to worthy causes. The question goes back to this: if we do not give the full ten percent of our income back to God, are we still being obedient and what blessings are we missing out on as the result?

By believing it is acceptable to be flexible in where we give our tithes, we have blurred the lines between tithing and gifts and offerings. We have also handicapped the ability of our local churches to serve those in need in organized outreaches, which has forced governments and agencies to try to adequately provide the care once provided by churches in the areas and ways most needed by the people in their own neighborhoods. Paying tithes as defined by the Bible will not only allow the local church to care more effectively for those around it but reduces the demand on governments they cannot meet as effectively or efficiently.

Tithes are tied to offerings in that both are money and resources given to God. The only difference between the two are tithes are the first ten percent of your resources, and offerings are anything given back to God above and beyond the ten percent. With either, resources are funneled through the church for either local expenses or mission outreaches. Offerings are sought whenever there is a special need, and there are numerous examples of those needs found throughout the Bible. We will only look at a few of them here, but there are more verses about offerings than there are for tithing.

Any time new plans for a worship center came through, or a new king restored worshipping the True God, the prophet or king sent out a nationwide request for offerings to cover the materials to build or rebuild the Tabernacle. The first example of this is found in Exodus 25:1-9 where "The Lord said to Moses, 'Tell the Israelites to bring me an offering. You are to receive the offering for me from everyone whose heart prompts them to give. These are the offerings you are to receive from them: gold, silver, and bronze; blue, purple, and scarlet yarn and fine linen; goat hair; ram skins dyed red and another type of durable leather; acacia wood; olive oil for the light; spices for the anointing oil and for the fragrant incense; and onyx stones and other gems to be mounted on the ephod and breastpiece. Then have them make a sanctuary for me, and I will dwell among them. Make this tabernacle and all its furnishings exactly like the pattern I will show you.'" Even though the original Tabernacle was highly mobile and made mostly of skins, it was still ornate in a country sort of style. It was put together by the finest craftsmen in the tribes and made to be dismantled every morning and set up every night as the Israelites traveled through the desert after they left Egypt.

The next request for an offering had a different intent. When Moses was on Mount Sinai for a longer time than the Israelites expected, they gave up hope and wanted something else to worship. Aaron's solution was to build them a golden calf, turning right back to idolatry as found in Exodus 32:2-4. "Aaron answered them, 'Take off the gold earrings that your wives, your sons, and your daughters are wearing, and bring them to me.' So all the people took off their earrings and brought them to Aaron. He took what they handed him and made it into an idol cast in the shape of a calf, fashioning it with a tool. Then they said, 'These are your gods, Israel, who brought you up out of Egypt.'" When Moses came down the mountain with the first Ten Commandments, the Israelites ended up drinking the powdered gold of the idol in their water and many of them died from the plague God sent because of their disobedience.

Once the Tabernacle was finished, there was a twelve-day dedication ceremony for it. Numbers 8 lists a series of offerings God told the Israelites to bring, from animals to sacrifice for their sins and tools made from precious metals to use for offerings to money for every male. These offerings provided the funds needed to establish the role of the priests serving in the temple, which was then maintained by the regular offerings

God set up in Deuteronomy. It is important to note the offerings were set to be progressive, as found in Deuteronomy 16:16-17 which says, "Three times a year all your men must appear before the Lord your God at the place he will choose: at the Festival of Unleavened Bread, the Festival of Weeks and the Festival of Tabernacles. No one should appear before the Lord empty-handed: Each of you must bring a gift in proportion to the way the Lord your God has blessed you." In other words, while it was ok for the poorest to bring an offering of a few cents and a dove, those who could afford it had to bring lambs and cows for offerings and an amount of money that reflected their wealth.

One place in the Bible you might think there was a large fundraising drive would be to fund the permanent temple in Jerusalem. There was not any fundraising or taxing involved to build it in Solomon's reign, and there is an important lesson for those who are constantly wanting new buildings, upgrades, or expansions and are willing to "pay" for them through debt or last-minute congregational pleas. It was heavy on King David's heart to build a permanent temple for God, but God told him he had killed too many people and to focus on building a house for himself in 2 Samuel 7. Even though God told David no, David did everything in his power to make the temple a reality. He set aside part of the taxes, gifts, plunder and tribute he received every year to pay for it. By the time Solomon started to build the temple all the money and precious metals were sitting in storehouses and Solomon only had to contract with kings who had forests to cut the wood he needed. If church builders took this approach today building programs wouldn't have such a bad reputation and more money would be available for outreach programs.

The New Testament continues along this line. While Jesus is recorded talking about the motives behind people giving, he avoided going into the specifics of the types. The topic comes up several times after Jesus left the Earth, however. Acts 21:26 says, "The next day Paul took the men and purified himself along with them. Then he went to the temple to give notice of the date when the days of purification would end and the offering would be made for each of them." This is a flashback to the Old Testament laws where people took oaths to do things for a specific amount of time, and the custom of giving an offering at the end of the oath. 2 Corinthians 8:19-21 says, "What is more, he was chosen by the churches to accompany us as we carry the offering, which we administer in order to honor the

Lord himself and to show our eagerness to help. We want to avoid any criticism of the way we administer this liberal gift. For we are taking pains to do what is right, not only in the eyes of the Lord but also in the eyes of man." It shows part of the money collected on Paul's journeys was to fund the church, but in addition extra was collected to support churches struggling with poverty. There are a few other references to offerings in the New Testament, but all show a difference between the tithe and offerings.

The last issue to discuss with offerings is indulgences. Although this was a well-established tradition in at least one denomination, there is not any Biblical support to the practice—at least in the versions of the Bible used by most denominations. As we will see in another chapter, money given to bias the decision of a person in a position of influence is a bribe. Indulgences were financial "offerings" given to improve the plight of loved ones after they died, despite the belief their sins have already been forgiven. If forgiveness is based on one's personal faith, death ends the possibility of changing their financial destination. God's message is focused on love, but He is also the God of Justice, and is dead set against taking bribes. Even though selling indulgences has been banned for centuries, the idea of God changing the punishment or reward of a person after they die because of gifts of money goes against the consistent character He demonstrates.

I chose to discuss tithes and offerings together because they are both money (and other resources) given to God through the local church. The difference between the two lies in the amount and the purpose. Tithes are the first ten percent of a person's livelihood given to support the church, and it is irrelevant if that comes as money or as part of their harvest. Offerings are resources people give voluntarily over and above the tithe and are generally given to support specific causes or ministries, such as food pantries or missions. Gifts do not fall under either of these categories and are discussed in the next chapter.

GIFTS

There are three types of giving mentioned in the Bible. The first is tithing, or recognizing God is the source of all we have and thankfully returning ten percent back to Him. The second type is offerings or giving more than ten percent back to God through the local church for special purposes. The third type is gifts, which is giving finances or other resources to those around us who are in need.

Before we discuss what gifts are, we need to look at the concept of compassion. Compassion is defined by Webster as "sympathetic pity and concern for the sufferings or misfortunes of others." It is important to understand compassion does not play a role in giving tithes and only a minor role in offerings since they are given back to God and, while they may work their way through systems and organizations to benefit those in need, they are received by churches or other religious organizations. Gifts, on the other hand, are targeted directly to specific needs and are given through compassion.

It is important to mention something compassion is not. Compassion is not feeling sorry for someone. It is easy to feel sorry for someone we see begging on the street corner. It is easy to feel sorry for an older lady struggling to push her grocery cart through the parking lot. It is easy to feel sorry for the outcast student eating by themselves in the corner while people talk about her. It is easy to feel sorry for a coworker trying to stay focused on his job while his marriage collapses. We can all think of people we feel sorry for, but it is not compassion until we care enough about that person to do something to make their situation better. Compassion is feeding the beggar a meal. Compassion is pushing the grocery cart to the person's car. Compassion is sitting with the outcast and becoming her friend. Compassion is listening to the coworker's story for the tenth time and giving him advice and support. Feeling sorry for people is the secular version of caring, while compassion is choosing to invest your time and possibly finances into someone's life.

One of the key differences between feeling sorry for someone and having compassion on them is a tendency to compare. We look at the beggar and feel sorry for them standing out in the cold or rain, then think if they would just get a job they wouldn't suffer from the weather. We look at the senior citizen and wonder why she does not have any family or friends to go shopping with her like we would. We whisper about the outcast in the corner—in a concerned, caring way—but think to ourselves if she just combed her hair and dressed in clean clothes, she would be accepted. We look at the coworker and think if he would just do the physical chores around the house and lose fifty pounds his wife would want to be around him. Once again, the greater the wealth gap between the person struggling and ourselves, the easier it is to pity them instead of being Jesus's hands and feet in showing compassion to them. At the same time if someone does help the person we are pitying, they are very likely to now or in the past be in a similar situation and are perfectly happy to totter around them in the same broken physical or emotional state to make their life slightly easier.

I am writing this two days after the Cathedral of Notre Dame burned in Paris, France. The most recent news update said over a billion dollars have been pledged by businesses and individuals worldwide to help France repair this religious and national landmark. The question that came to mind is this: does that money qualify as offerings or gifts? The cause is to rebuild a very old cathedral that has housed religious artifacts for centuries, so for some what they gave would qualify as offerings. On the other hand, donors cross religious and international lines so those who give to restore a national landmark qualify as gifts. In other words, just as I was trying to draw clear lines between the types of giving from a religious perspective, God throws a curve ball to prove there are exceptions to any human rule. Instead of taking the approach of the Pharisees and creating more and more rules to cover every base, I choose to shrug my shoulders and go back to the reality of your heart defining your relationship with, and how you show appreciation towards, God.

The first reference to gifts is found in Gen 25:52-53 which says, "When Abraham's servant heard what they said, he bowed down to the ground before the Lord. Then the servant brought out gold and silver jewelry and articles of clothing and gave them to Rebekah; he also gave costly gifts to her brother and to her mother. Then he and the men who were with him ate and drank and spent the night there." The first mention of gifts was Abraham's servant using his master's wealth to attract the attention of the father of Isaac's future bride. This happened before negotiations began over the dowry, so if he had chosen the wrong woman, he could have squandered his master's wealth. However, since he listened to God everything fell into place and he returned home with a beautiful woman with a great personality and work ethic to continue his master's family line.

Deuteronomy 15:10-11 gives the next example of how to give gifts when it says, "Give generously to them and do so without a grudging heart; then because of this the Lord your God will bless you in all your work and in everything you put your hand to. There will always be poor people in the land. Therefore I command you to be openhanded toward your fellow Israelites who are poor and needy in your land." This shows gifts are to be given directly to people, but still fall in the realm of having a religious basis since they were focused towards people of the same nationality. This reflects back to how you should prioritize your finances, emphasizing you should care for your family and neighbors before reaching further beyond your borders.

The next type of gift is found in 1 Samuel 25:26-17 which says, " And now, my lord, as surely as the Lord your God lives and as you live, since the Lord has kept you from bloodshed and from avenging yourself with your own hands, may your enemies and all who are intent on harming my lord be like Nabal. And let this gift, which your servant has brought to my lord, be given to the men who follow you." This is from the story of David being dishonored by Nabal after guarding his sheep for months. David asked Nabal to let his men eat with the herders during the festival where he sheared the sheep, and Nabal broke both custom and respect by refusing to let them participate. David's response was to arm his men and head towards his house to deliver justice, but Nabal's wife Abigail heard what was going and went to meet David with a feast for his men. In this case the gifts she brought were to repay a wrong and gain back honor for their family. It succeeded so well that David married Abigail after she became a widow days after the sheepshearing was over. This type of gift is supported in Proverbs 21:1 which tells us, "A gift given in secret soothes anger, and a bribe concealed in the cloak pacifies great wrath."

The next type of gift is found in 1 Kings 10:10 which says, "And she gave the king 120 talents of gold, large quantities of spices, and precious stones. Never again were so many spices brought in as those the queen of Sheba gave to King Solomon." There the Queen of Sheba brings great wealth as a sign of respect to King Solomon when she traveled to meet him after finding out the stories of his wisdom were true. King Solomon honored her wisdom and interest shortly after by sending back a large amount of wealth from his treasury when she left. Both individuals were equally wealthy, so the point was not to win influence. We could compare this exchange to something like exchanging Christmas presents, signs of respect between peers without ulterior motives.

The giving of gifts to show respect is found again in 1 Kings 10:24-25 which says, "The whole world sought audience with Solomon to hear the wisdom God had put in his heart. Year after year, everyone who came brought a gift—articles of silver and gold, robes, weapons and spices, and horses and mules." Here people who came to see King Solomon brought a gift out of respect. There are many verses which show this custom was observed when people went to a prophet to have a question answered or ritual performed. While giving gifts to the king were not significant to him economically, to a prophet it provided necessary food and money to live as they carried out their duties. This was demonstrated again in 2 Kings 5 where the general visited Naaman to be healed of leprosy. The reason for the gift was the same, to show respect to the office. This is clarified in Pro 18:16 which says, "A gift opens the way and ushers the giver into the presence of the great." This is the type of gifts the Magi offered to baby Jesus when they had followed the star to his house that is found in Matthew 2:11 which states, "On coming to the house, they saw the child with his mother Mary, and they bowed down and worshiped him. Then they opened their treasures and presented him with gifts of gold, frankincense and myrrh."

Giving gifts to those who have survived tragedy is another type of gift described in the Bible. Ezra 1:4, 6 says, "And in any locality where survivors may now be living, the people are to provide them with silver and gold, with goods and livestock, and with freewill offerings for the temple of God in Jerusalem.' All their neighbors assisted them with articles of silver and gold, with goods and livestock, and with valuable gifts, in addition to all the freewill offerings." Here the tragedy described was the Israelites being dispersed from their homeland for political reasons. The same concept can be applied to natural disasters and health issues as well. This ties back into how churches cared for the sick and poor for centuries before the government became involved. When Christians immediately care for those around them in unexpected circumstances the care is faster, more efficient, and far less likely to develop into dependence.

It is important to remember the ultimate gift ever made was God sending Jesus to die on the cross. As Paul put it in Romans 5:15-17, "But the gift is not like the trespass. For if the many died by the trespass of the one man, how much more did God's grace and the gift that came by the grace of the one man, Jesus Christ, overflow to the many! Nor can the gift of God be compared with the result of one man's sin: The judgment followed one sin and brought condemnation, but the gift followed many trespasses and brought justification. For if, by the trespass of the one man, death reigned through that one man, how much more will those who receive God's abundant provision of grace and of the gift of righteousness reign in life through the one man, Jesus Christ!" One man (or woman, depending on your viewpoint—you can fight that out amongst yourselves) brought sin into the world by eating the forbidden fruit. One gift, Jesus dying on the cross, removed not only that sin but the sin of millions since the Garden of Eden who have asked for it. From a realistic viewpoint, no matter how extravagant of a gift we give, it is insignificant in value compared to what God gave to us to restore our relationship with Him.

Our giving should reflect the selfless act God showed to us when He gave His son to die in our place. 1 John 3:16-18 tells us, "This is how we know what love is: Jesus Christ laid down his life for us. And we ought to lay down our lives for our brothers and sisters. If anyone has material possessions and sees a brother or sister in need but has no pity on them, how can the love of God be in that person? Dear children, let us not love with words or speech but with actions and in truth." Talking about good means nothing, which is the downfall of many social justice activists now. It is common for many to have monthly meetings to discuss the evils of the world found in the latest headlines, maybe organize a fundraiser for them, then jump to whatever new issue is making the news. The true spirit of giving is to give until it hurts, and the problem is significantly addressed instead of being concerned about being on the front pages giving superficial attention to the latest cause, chasing the headlines instead of demonstrating honest compassion and long-term giving.

The second most important gift ever given is when God released the Holy Spirit onto the earth. This is described in Hebrews 6:4-6 which says, "It is impossible for those who have once been enlightened, who have tasted the heavenly gift, who have shared in the Holy Spirit, who have tasted the goodness of the word of God and the powers of the coming age and who have fallen away, to be brought back to repentance. To their loss they are crucifying the Son of God all over again and subjecting him to public disgrace." This is a topic which many books have been written about, but here is a quick overview. The Holy Spirit is a person, the third member of the Trinity. He is present everywhere with everyone, and initially leads a person to accept Jesus Christ's gift to atone from their sin. After someone repents, the Holy Spirit assumes a role of teacher and mentor to guide them to a better understanding of their relationship with God, and to grow their spiritual gifts to help not only themselves but those around them deepen that relationship. At some point the person will come to the realization they are not in control of their lives and cannot eliminate habits and urges they know are sinful, at which point they can choose to allow the Holy Spirit to have control of their lives. They will never be perfect, but taking this step dramatically changes how their relationship with God interacts with the world. It is at this point many people obtain the Gift of Tongues, or a heavenly language which enables them to communicate more effectively with God through prayer.

There are inappropriate ways to give gifts as well. As usual, the gift is rarely wrong. What makes it inappropriate is the intent and motivations of either the giver or receiver. Here are a few examples of when you should reconsider giving gifts, even when it is either socially expected or there is significant peer pressure to do it.

The first instance is when the gift is given with the expectation of receiving something in return. Although this takes on many forms, when someone does this, they are guilty of bribery. Attempting to get something through financial, political, or social manipulation eliminates the aspect of compassion from the gift so it invalidates the gesture in principle. It also eliminates it as a show of respect since it is an attempt to leverage something to benefit yourself. There are many verses that deal with this subject, so I will list several to show the different aspects of selfishness they cover.

Numbers 22:16-18 They came to Balaam and said: "This

is what Balak son of Zippor says: Do not let anything keep you from coming to me, because I will reward you handsomely and do whatever you say. Come and put a curse on these people for me." But Balaam answered them, "Even if Balak gave me all the silver and gold in his palace, I could not do anything great or small to go beyond the command of the Lord my God.

Deuteronomy 27:25 "Cursed is anyone who accepts a bribe to kill an innocent person." Then all the people shall say, "Amen!"

Judges 16:4-5 Some time later, he fell in love with a woman in the Valley of Sorek whose name was Delilah. The rulers of the Philistines went to her and said, "See if you can lure him into showing you the secret of his great strength and how we can overpower him so we may tie him up and subdue him. Each one of us will give you eleven hundred shekels of silver."

1 Samuel 8:1-3 When Samuel grew old, he appointed his sons as Israel's leaders. The name of his firstborn was Joel and the name of his second was Abijah, and they served at Beersheba. But his sons did not follow his ways. They turned aside after dishonest gain and accepted bribes and perverted justice.

Esther 4:7 Mordecai told him everything that had happened to him, including the exact amount of money Haman had promised to pay into the royal treasury for the destruction of the Jews.

Proverbs 17:8 A bribe is seen as a charm by the one who gives it; they think success will come at every turn.

Ecclesiastes 7:7 Extortion turns a wise person into a fool, and a bribe corrupts the heart.

Micah 3:11 Her leaders judge for a bribe, her priests teach for a price, and her prophets tell fortunes for money.

Yet they look for the Lord's support and say, "Is not the Lord among us? No disaster will come upon us."

Habakkuk 2:6-9 Will not all of them taunt him with ridicule and scorn, saying, "Woe to him who piles up stolen goods and makes himself wealthy by extortion! How long must this go on?" Will not your creditors suddenly arise? Will they not wake up and make you tremble? Then you will become their prey. Because you have plundered many nations, the peoples who are left will plunder you. For you have shed human blood; you have destroyed lands and cities and everyone in them. Woe to him who builds his house by unjust gain, setting his nest on high to escape the clutches of ruin!

Acts 8:18-24 When Simon saw that the Spirit was given at the laying on of the apostles' hands, he offered them money and said, "Give me also this ability so that everyone on whom I lay my hands may receive the Holy Spirit." Peter answered: "May your money perish with you, because you thought you could buy the gift of God with money! You have no part or share in this ministry, because your heart is not right before God. Repent of this wickedness and pray to the Lord in the hope that he may forgive you for having such a thought in your heart. For I see that you are full of bitterness and captive to sin." Then Simon answered, "Pray to the Lord for me so that nothing you have said may happen to me."

Another mistake when giving is to value the gift instead of the relationship. It is appropriate and wise to give something of lower value to distant relatives and friends, such as giving a Kitchen-Aide mixer to your sibling for their wedding while giving your coworker a set of barbeque tools. It is wrong and highly inappropriate to give the coworker a Kitchen-Aide mixer and expect them to treat you differently or give you credit for things you did not do as a result. Matthew 23:16-22 puts it, "Woe to you, blind guides! You say, 'If anyone swears by the temple, it means nothing; but anyone who swears by the gold of the temple is bound by that oath.' You blind fools! Which is greater: the gold, or the temple that makes the gold sacred? You also say, 'If anyone swears by the altar, it means nothing; but anyone who swears by the gift on the altar is bound by that oath.' You blind men! Which is greater: the gift, or the altar that makes the gift sacred? Therefore, anyone who swears by the altar swears by it and by everything on it. And anyone who swears by the temple swears by it and by the one who dwells in it. And anyone who swears by heaven swears by God's throne and by the one who sits on it." Giving a gift you value more highly than your relationship with a person in attempt to get something from them once again qualifies as a bribe and must be avoided.

Giving a gift to someone to salve your conscience instead of paying them for their work is also an abuse of giving. Romans 4:4-5 says, "Now to the one who works, wages are not credited as a gift but as an obligation. However, to the one who does not work but trusts God who justifies the ungodly, their faith is credited as righteousness." This is a frequent area of abuse in churches and social groups. If someone you know makes their living as a carpenter, it is fine to occasionally ask their advice about projects if they tell you they do not mind giving it. However, it is an abuse of their time and livelihood for you to expect them to come and volunteer away from their work to help you with your weekend warrior project. If they volunteer to help you without any pressure, then it is appropriate to give them a gift in recognition of their position and expertise in return. If they are struggling financially or are in the middle of numerous projects, you should pay them if they assist you. No matter the type of work you need, from an attorney to a hairdresser to a concrete job to financial expertise, it is not appropriate for you to expect the expert you know to help you out without fairly compensating them.

Another mistake people make when giving gifts is to do the bare minimum. What I mean by this is, they give enough to qualify as being generous, but it does not match either the need or their ability to give. We are called to be generous, not stingy. This is discussed in 2 Corinthians 9:6-15 which says, "Remember this: Whoever sows sparingly will also reap sparingly, and whoever sows generously will also reap generously. Each of you should give what you have decided in your heart to give, not reluctantly or under compulsion, for God loves a cheerful giver. And God is able to bless you abundantly, so that in all things at all times, having all that you need, you will abound in every good work. As it is written: 'They have freely scattered their gifts to the poor; their righteousness endures forever.' Now he who supplies seed to the sower and bread for food will also supply and increase your store of seed and will enlarge the harvest of your righteousness. You will be enriched in every way so that you can be generous on every occasion, and through us your generosity will result in thanksgiving to God. This service that you perform is not only supplying the needs of the Lord's people but is also overflowing in many expressions of thanks to God. Because of the service by which you have proved yourselves, others will praise God for the obedience that accompanies your confession of the gospel of Christ, and for your generosity in sharing with them and with everyone else. And in their prayers for you their hearts will go out to you, because of the surpassing grace God has given you. Thanks be to God for his indescribable gift!" It's a long passage, but it gives the basics of how to give once you commit to a cause.

The last way to err in giving is supporting causes that can support themselves. This is mentioned in 2 Corinthians 11:7-9 where Paul says, "Was it a sin for me to lower myself in order to elevate you by preaching the gospel of God to you free of charge? I robbed other churches by receiving support from them so as to serve you. And when I was with you and needed something, I was not a burden to anyone, for the brothers who came from Macedonia supplied what I needed. I have kept myself from being a burden to you in any way and will continue to do so." This would be the equivalent of church planters raising support when they open a new work, which is necessary for them to have time necessary to establish themselves in the community. However, church planters should not be given a never-ending blank check. Part of building a new church is teaching and building a giving program (tithes and offerings) which will fully support themselves within three to five years. There are many nonprofit organizations which will never support themselves, but in all cases, organizations should focus on being efficient and goal-oriented to prevent wasteful spending and build long-term resources to accomplish their goals.

Many times people feel obligated to give to every cause that comes their way. Out of habit they write a check for a minimal amount, trying to get into all the action (and blessings). If we took this approach to car maintenance we would have one new tire, one new headlight, the dents repaired in the rear fender and new wax on the hood while one wheel well is rusted out, the other tail light burned out, a door handle missing on the passenger side and the rear window covered with plastic. Here are a few thoughts on how to not only give Biblically, but effectively as well:

First, make sure the cause is legitimate. There are thousands of scams out there, some focused on the religious community. While many of these are dressed up in heart-wrenching clothes, a little research will reveal their weaknesses. One example is the Black Lives Matter movement. Before anyone becomes offended, it is obvious there are issues with economies, criminal organizations, political machines, and educational opportunities in the ghettos of most large cities. On the other hand, there are other suburbs in large cities full of non-white residents with adequate education, high employment, and decent wages who have average crime rates without additional funding or grants based on race. Black Lives Matter started with a racial crime which turned out to be false, created websites and brochures which outrageously misquoted facts taken out of context and used fringe leaders to intimidate companies and organizations into making donations on threats of political and legal action. After all the hoopla died down, the reality of the birthplace of the movement turned out to be a culture of single parents, gang membership, inept politicians in power for decades and a culture where attending school and doing homework was severely discouraged. The problem was not white cops randomly shooting innocent blacks, but a culture discouraging most behaviors necessary for a peaceful economy. Never jump on a bandwagon without closely examining if the cause is valid and the proposed solution will actually solve the problem.

Next, create a list of what you care about. Do this by making a list of what burns your heart. If the cause that keeps you up at night is educating orphans in Africa caused by the AIDS epidemic, throwing a few dollars at United Way that supports causes such as Planned Parenthood would go against your passion. If feeding the homeless is what lights your fire then the Gideons should not be on high on your donors list. If teaching third world nations how to feed themselves occupies your mind then you should cross organizations focused on social justice off your list. Not only should you live and work your passion, you should carry it through to your giving as well. Focus on what is important to you. This allows you to give significantly more to advance the causes you care about instead of giving insignificant amounts to everything that walks through your door.

The last step to successful gift giving is to set up a line item in your budget for it. This does not include the ten percent tithe you give to support your local church, but is an additional amount, say one to five percent of your income, you will use to support causes. Part of that can be dedicated as a monthly amount to something such as KLOVE or AirOne radio, while the rest remains undesignated for a neighbor who is laid off, the beggar on the street corner or someone God impresses on your heart at church. By setting aside a specific amount every month you will have money available to support the causes important to you and those you find in your community. This does not mean you are limited to only giving this amount, but it is taking ownership of fulfilling your moral obligation to those beyond your own family.

Who knew talking about giving gifts could be so complicated? It is not really that bad, but there are a lot of ways to think about giving that may not have crossed your mind before. If your goal with gifting is to get attention for how often or much you give, then you are a failure at giving. If your purpose is gifting with compassion for the causes closest to your heart, then you need to focus on giving more to your passions and not get distracted with everything that crosses your path with its hand out. By setting aside an amount each month to give and doing your homework to make sure the causes you support are valid and accomplishing their goals, the value of your giving can increase exponentially by leveraging your efforts for both local needs and effective international organizations.

Figure 2

TYPES OF RELIGIOUS GIVING

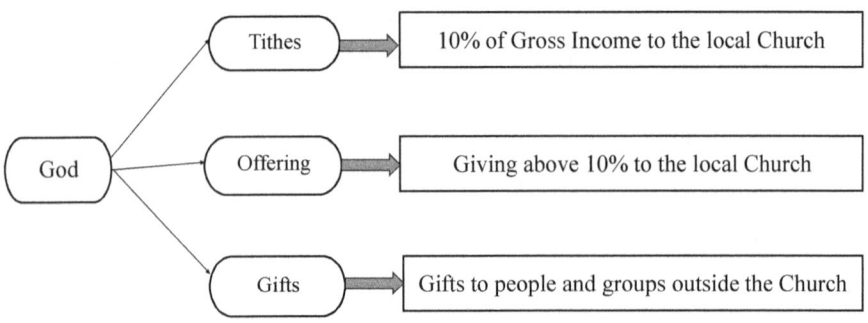

MONEY IS NEUTRAL

There are two opposing schools of thought about money in Christianity today. One is money is evil. The other is if you are a good Christian you will be rewarded financially to the point you will be wealthy, or at least well off. While both ideologies are popular, the reality is they are both wrong. Why they are wrong lies in the same thought process, and both approaches use fear to convince people to use them. Since a true relationship with Christ is based on love and respect, both schools of thought must be rejected.

Many conservative Christian organizations teach money is evil. It is summed up in the misquotation of 1 Timothy 6:10 when they say, "For money is the root of all evil." If this were true, everyone who works spends a large part of their lives chasing after something evil. Those who live by this motto are miserable, because in all but the most primitive cultures one must have money to feed, clothe and protect themselves and their families. If it were true then the Bible spends a significant amount of time supporting the use of something evil, and even encouraging every able-bodied person to earn it.

This wrong belief leads to a life a fear. There is a fear of earning too much. There is a fear of not giving enough. There is the fear of using it for the wrong thing. There is a fear of living too extravagantly. There is a fear of using too much of it on yourself or your family. There is a fear of being selfish if you save for the future. These fears can snowball as you face everyday situations and have led many to regret their lack of planning when they failed to set aside enough money to cover major car and home repairs and health issues. This results in a meager retirement and needing financial assistance to cover any major health or repair issues.

What the verse really says is, "For the love of money is a root of all kinds of evil. Some people, eager for money, have wandered from the faith and pierced themselves with many griefs." Money is not the problem. The problem is greed and materialism. When humans place the pursuit and use of money above their dedication for God, they can easily become sidetracked into other sins as they pursue it. If money is not evil, then it is not something we should be afraid of and, like everything else, learn how to use it effectively.

The other popular approach to money in Christianity is believing a strong faith will result in financial wealth. It is found in many forms, the least strident of which is if you have a valid faith in Christ you will at least have enough—enough to pay your bills, enough to cover repairs to your car and home, enough to pay for health care emergencies, enough to cover basic necessities such as food and utilities, etc. Commonly called the "Health and Wealth" doctrine, it has also been misnamed the "Prosperity Doctrine," which a later chapter demonstrates is an integral part of the financial teachings in the Bible but does not promise wealth. Whichever version of it you choose to focus on, it does not accurately represent what is taught in the Bible.

While the list of fears stemming from the belief money is evil is long and can be paralyzing, the fears coming from this philosophy can be even worse. I have talked to several people in a financial crisis who were having a massive religious crisis they believed came from not having enough faith in God. I believe it also is partially responsible for an unofficial caste system in so-called Christian countries where those who make the least are rejected and/or pitied by those who make more based on a theoretical religious issue instead of issues rooted in a lack of education and opportunity. This is also reflected on the other side as the poor give a higher percentage of their income to various religious causes in an attempt to earn God's favor to earn the right belief status, and also in the resigned religious hopelessness of generations who have given up trying to reach a higher economic status because no one in their family has managed to break into that elusive category of having enough. While it is key for a Christian to have a clear understanding of both the source of wealth and the correct priorities, education and opportunity plays a far greater role in improving their economic status than simple religious sincerity.

These opposing viewpoints also play an important role in why churches and organizations can spend decades in missionary outreaches to poor nations without causing significant impacts on their economic qualities of life. If the group believes money is evil, they will focus on evangelism and distributing the cast-off gifts of their supporters, with moderate effort going towards bettering their food and water supplies so they will not corrupt that culture with greed and materialism. If the group believes increased wealth is based on faith in God, they will again focus on evangelism and establishing religious support groups to improve the culture's belief level so they will eventually "earn" wealth through religious fervor. Both approaches contradict how the most effective religious and secular outreach groups operate, which is to identify and improve an economic or health need which creates interest within those cultures to understand the religious beliefs of those who dramatically impacted their lives.

These approaches to wealth also play roles in how governments try to solve social problems in their own countries, including the United States. If money is evil, the answer can never be funding groups or local organizations directly because they would inevitably be biased, wasteful or wrongfully influenced by local connections or payoffs to not spend the money efficiently. If wealth is strictly based on personal faith, then it does not matter how much money you spend to fix an economic issue because it will not make any difference until a religious event (usually called a revival) occurs to raise that culture's wealth worthiness. If issues are caused by a lack of education, opportunity, and technology, then the government will invest in organizations who focus on specific needs unique to each area with funding and, as those issues are resolved, the economy will improve and resources can then be reassigned to the next most pressing issue.

Figure 3

RANK IN ORDER OF HAZARD

$50.00 Bill

Colt 45 Revolver

Cell Phone with Internet

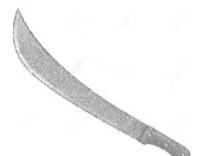

Machete

Fentanyl Tablets

I want you to picture in your mind a table with a white tablecloth on it. A row of objects lies down the middle of the table. Those objects are a $50 bill, a Colt 45 revolver, a cell phone with an active internet connection, a machete, and a bottle with Fentanyl tablets in it. Rank those objects from the most dangerous to the least. Now think about why you ranked them in that order. The reality is all of them are harmless. They will all sit there on that table forever doing absolutely nothing unless someone picks them up. When someone picks one up it has an equal capacity of being used for good or evil, but the use lies entirely in the purpose and intent of the person who uses it.

While it is common for denominations to blame objects for how they are used, objects are innocent of all motives and actions. It is easier to blame objects than to admit personal responsibility. It is even easier to rationalize how we consider using objects as good even when we know what we use them for are not fulfilling God's purposes. Proverbs 16:2 says, "All a person's ways seem pure to them, but motives are weighed by the Lord." You can use the $50 bill on the table to buy ammunition for the revolver which you use to kill an animal for food and skin it with the machete. On the other hand, you can buy the same ammunition and use the revolver and machete to injure or kill people. In either example the money, gun, and knife remain innocent while the person using them defines the morality of their use.

It is important to remember money is a neutral tool that reflects the values of the person using it. As a tool it is important to learn the most effective way to use it from professionals. At the same time, it is important to recognize God is the source of your income and put Him and His values first. By balancing the right priorities with proven techniques, you will learn how to become prosperous so you can care for your family and be increasingly generous with those around you.

THE CONCEPT OF VALUE

One big consequence of focusing on Now instead of the Source is losing the ability to distinguish between a need and a want. When most of the earthly wealth becomes concentrated in a handful of countries, the immense wealth available to everyone in those nations means luxuries are available to everyone while millions in the rest of the world are without basic needs. That wealth also leads to carelessness and a lack of appreciation, which is one reason why the average American throws away a third of the food they buy while people within a few hundred miles suffer from starvation. This does not mean those who can afford luxury items should adopt subsistence lifestyles. It does mean we should all become more conscientious of what we have and buy so we can redirect what we now waste to improve the health and lifestyles of those who currently do without.

Webster defines need as "the lack of the means of subsistence." Subsistence is a concept few can realistically imagine anymore, and the technology and wealth we acquire makes it difficult to accept. Subsistence is not something affected by race, culture, or wealth. In its most basic form, it is having enough food to sustain health, clothing to protect from the elements and housing to provide a safe and comfortable place to live. If everyone focused on these three issues, over a third of the economy of the United States would be eliminated, along with many luxuries we think we must have to survive. Here is a short list of necessities compared to what we have convinced ourselves we must have to be successful:

Figure 4

WANTS VS. NEEDS

Issue	Need	Want
Shelter	Tent or cabin	McMansion
Food	Garden, hunting or farm	McDonalds
Clothing	Overalls, flour sack dresses	Ripped jeans, fashion statement
Communication	Talking	Cell phone, computer
Transportation	Walking, horse	Ferrari
Entertainment	Tag, community events	Movies, video games
Vacation	Visiting family	Cruises, trips overseas

Webster defines value as "a fair return or equivalent in goods, services, or money for something exchanged." What is inherent in the definition is the value of something is different for each person. That is why going to an auction, especially one for an estate, can be so fascinating. A rusty old tool may seem worthless to most people in the crowd, but to one bidder it could be the last piece of a collection they will pay hundreds of dollars for. Some people fight for a TV on sale during Black Friday they would ignore every other day of the year because the lower price suddenly makes the technology desirable. There are many times I will walk by an item in the grocery store without any interest in it, but when it goes on sale, I will buy it and try it out of curiosity. New cars can sit on the lot for months until they go on sale at the year-end when people will buy all available within days.

The difference in value becomes even more dramatic when you look across countries and cultures. The Ferrari people admire so much in the United States would be worthless to an African tribe who travel by foot down paths created by their ancestors. A parka is almost a necessity in Minnesota but might only be useful as a canopy in Arizona. If you believe the ads, a 3D television could make or break your Super Bowl party in California but at best be a computer monitor in Brazil, in areas where cable and satellite are not available. Even basic accessories like a shower are only worthless decorations in places that do not have running water.

Money is probably where we err the most in trusting for its value. It is simply paper and bits of metal worth a few pennies at best, and we are rapidly transitioning into invisible ones and zeros racing through cyberspace between banks. While some church denominations have panicked for years about a chip implanted in a person being the mark of the beast, we are rapidly moving towards societies where a small microprocessor under the skin will not only transfer money but also give instant identification and medical records access no matter where in the world we are. (As a side note, I would say the concept of the microprocessor being the mark of the beast is outdated since security and access permissions are already controlled through servers for credit cards and instant check readers.) Anyone who tries to isolate themselves from this massive shift in technology will soon find themselves bartering for necessities and fighting for a shrinking number of doctors providing medical care off the books.

An individual's sense of value becomes more skewed as the level of cultural industrialization increases. "Primitive" cultures place the most value on religion, family, and survival, while some in "advanced" cultures expect the government and charities to care for those who struggle. Someone from an isolated Amazon tribe would probably use a $100 bill to start a fire, while that same piece of paper might start a riot in the middle of a Wal-Mart in Colorado. A person in California might spend ten times what it would cost for health insurance for their family on a car while leaving their family unprotected. Someone in Washington might spend more annually for a home security system than they donate to the local homeless shelter. While technology may reduce the amount of physical work we have to do, it also isolates us from the land and people around us that provide the necessities of life.

As the perceived value of things change, so does their cost. This is why the stock market is a roller coaster, influenced more by emotion than economics. The cost of pharmacy stock can increase if someone suggests they are on the verge of releasing a new drug or medical aid, or plummet if a clinical trial gives inconclusive data, or their CEO triples the price of a medication without cause. This is nothing new, however. We find this happening in Samaria in 2 Kings 6 and 7. Ben-Hadad laid siege to the city for so long you had to pay eighty shekels of silver to buy a donkey head because food was so scarce. Then Elisha called for God's help after the king sought deliverance from the right Source, and the next day you could buy enough of the finest flour to bake bread for one shekel. Today you could compare it to the value of one share of Enron the day before and after their corrected financial statements were released. In both instances the substance itself remained the same, but the perception of their values changed dramatically.

There are several verses in the Bible that remind us wealth and possessions are not the meaning of life and draw us back to the Source. Psalms 19:9-10 tells us, "The fear of the Lord is pure, enduring forever. The decrees of the Lord are firm, and all of them are righteous. They are more precious than gold, than much pure gold; they are sweeter than honey, than honey from the honeycomb." Psalms 119:72 puts it like this, "The law from your mouth is more precious to me than thousands of pieces of silver and gold." Proverbs 10:20 makes it personal when it says, "The tongue of the righteous is choice silver, but the heart of the wicked is of little value." The theme continues in Proverbs 11:22, Proverbs 27:21, Ecclesiastes 7:11-12, Jeremiah 6:27-30, Lamentations 4:1-2 and many others.

The theme is found in the New Testament as well. Perhaps the verses that best sum up the Christian approach to value are 2 Timothy 2:20-21 which state, "In a large house there are articles not only of gold and silver, but also of wood and clay; some are for special purposes and some for common use. Those who cleanse themselves from the latter will be instruments for special purposes, made holy, useful to the Master and prepared to do any good work." There are all kinds of things made out of all kinds of materials. What something is made from is basically irrelevant. The value of "things" come from what they are used for. An old, rusty pickup truck used to help move people and haul yard waste for volunteers has more value than a Lamborghini someone squeals their tires in and arrogantly looks out at less expensive vehicles. A plastic fork used once to feed volunteers cleaning up a neighborhood after a flood is more valuable than the most expensive silver service polished daily in a house only used part of the year. The elaborate golden communion set in a church whose goal is to entertain people is less valuable than a chewed-up frisbee in the yard of a foster parent with a dog.

If it is so easy to have the wrong value system in a society chasing all the wrong things, what should we avoid? There is a long and varied list, so to satisfy the bullet point-obsessed here is a short one to start with. Some might look suspiciously like items found in another chapter, but don't worry, they can be used in either instance:

1. Categorize every purchase you made last month, then rank them by how many purchases you made and the total amount spent in each category. Based on the ranking, what are the most important things in your life?

2. Do you spend more of your "free" time on family and religious activities or on work and recreation?

3. What do you enjoy doing the most? (This is kind of a trick question, because there may be issues you need counseling to help resolve in families.)

4. If you could write a check for a million dollars right now, who would it be to?

5. If someone gave you a check for a million dollars right now, what would you spend it on?

6. If God told you to make a donation right now, who do you think it would be to?

7. Who is taking up the most of your time, and who gave them permission to have that much control over your life?

8. If you were forced to change places with a person in a culture the opposite of where you live now, how would that affect your life?

9. Look at the "stuff" you surround yourself with and honestly evaluate how much or little it contributes to what should have the highest priorities in your life.

10. Look at all the pieces of paper that surround us every day and rate the importance of them. An example would be a $100 bill vs. a handmade card from your child.

Making that list just made my head hurt because of all the little things I can think of that pull away from what is important. The sad part is, we often recognize the small nagging things we let distract us and let the big ugly things accepted by society fly along unquestioned. They are issues that have existed almost since man was created, so have become more difficult to recognize and deal with. As someone once said, always make the main thing the main thing. By focusing on the main things and handling the big issues, most of the small nagging things will be taken care of along the way.

As I was reading through the news today an article caught my eye. The headline was about a wealthy preacher of a megachurch buying a jet. In the article the pastor said having a jet was necessary to keep on top of things in his worldwide ministry. That is an argument any CEO of a multinational business can make convincingly. Then the article noted the ministry already had four other jets. That seems excessive for a religious organization. However, the next part turned out to be the controversial segment. In an interview, the minister said the reason he needed a private jet was not to have rapid access to his ministries and shuttle resources between them. The reason he said he needed another private jet was that people on commercial flights kept interrupting his sermon prep and prayer time for mundane prayer requests and asking for spiritual advice. This is a prime example of having something good for all the wrong reasons. While speaking is an integral part of his calling, putting it above the basic needs of caring for individual sheep is a major mistake. Being wealthy and spending money for business priorities is fine unless the money is spent for the wrong priorities. While I understand it must be frustrating to be a spiritual target because of your position and popularity, it is a part of the job description. I wonder how many times those people he did not want to care for were sent by God to enforce or redirect the message he was to deliver at the speaking engagement he was headed for.

The core of understanding the value of anything is the concept of contentment. The American and world economies have become experts at making things slightly bigger, faster, or more entertaining and convincing millions of people to spend hundreds of dollars every few months for that slight improvement. If our focus is on having the "best," latest, or unique (even though there is typically at least one person within a mile of us with the exact same thing), spending another $500 on a new phone after six months is reasonable, even though we do without health insurance or saving for retirement. Adding thousands of dollars in debt every one to three years for a new car is an acceptable part of life if our focus is on keeping up with the Joneses or impressing others.

On the other hand, if we understand our personal value lies in having a vibrant relationship with God and caring for others, "stuff" becomes far less important to us. The phone is no longer important as a status symbol because its value comes from keeping in contact with people and caring for their needs. The value of the car no longer comes from how new or what features it has and is derived from using it to transport those who need it or take necessities to those who cannot afford them. Church attendance and giving is not about making an appearance and impressing people but being spiritually fed and funding ways to help others.

Philippians 4:12-13 hits the core when Paul writes, "I know what it is to be in need, and I know what it is to have plenty. I have learned the secret of being content in any and every situation, whether well fed or hungry, whether living in plenty or in want. I can do all this through him who gives me strength." The most important key is to accept and be content in our present situation, no matter what it is. Stuff comes and goes. Tastes change. Even needs vary over time, especially after retirement. By making God the main thing, we can pursue and release the things and still maintain joy and contentment because we have our priorities straight.

1 Timothy 6:6-8 reminds us of how temporary life is when it says, "But godliness with contentment is great gain. For we brought nothing into the world, and we can take nothing out of it. But if we have food and clothing, we will be content with that." All the stuff is temporary things to enjoy, but our focus should always be on our relationship with God. Solomon had the right perspective when he wrote in Proverbs 30:7-9 "Two things I ask of you, Lord; do not refuse me before I die: Keep falsehood and lies far from me; give me neither poverty nor riches, but give me only my daily bread. Otherwise, I may have too much and disown you and say, 'Who is the Lord?' Or I may become poor and steal, and so dishonor the name of my God." His words proved accurate as his wealth and position led to many wives, who whispered the falsehoods of idols into his ears until they distracted him from the important things of life.

Not valuing things correctly leads to several other sins. Focusing on the things instead of God and others tempts us away from planning ahead and prioritizing the important things into giving others mastery over ourselves through debt as we pursue our thirst for instant gratification. The more distracted we allow ourselves to be, the easier it is for us to lose our focus and cut corners to get stuff we do not appreciate.

The first issue is coveting. Webster defines coveting as "to desire (what belongs to another) inordinately or culpably." Wanting to have more is a healthy part of the psyche, as previously mentioned in this book. What is dangerous and sinful is wanting to take something from someone else without putting in the time and effort to earn it for yourself. In fact, it made the Top Ten Commandments in Deuteronomy 5:21, which says, "You shall not covet your neighbor's wife. You shall not set your desire on your neighbor's house or land, his male or female servant, his ox or donkey, or anything that belongs to your neighbor." In other words, coveting goes far beyond wealth or possessions and plays a role in many divorces and suicides. It caused an entire family to be wiped out when someone coveted some plunder during one war in Joshua 7:20-25. Paul covers it in Rom 7:7-12 when he says, "What shall we say, then? Is the law sinful? Certainly not! Nevertheless, I would not have known what sin was had it not been for the law. For I would not have known what coveting really was if the law had not said, 'You shall not covet.' But sin, seizing the opportunity afforded by the commandment, produced in me every kind of coveting. For apart from the law, sin was dead. Once I was alive apart from the law; but when the commandment came, sin sprang to life and I died. I found that the very commandment that was intended to bring life actually brought death. For sin, seizing the opportunity afforded by the commandment, deceived me, and through the commandment put me to death. So then, the law is holy, and the commandment is holy, righteous, and good." Coveting is a mental issue, but if you do not stop the desire, it turns into action with spiritual consequences.

You may see something and not necessarily want to have it but develop a jealousy of the person that does. That is called envy and is as dangerous as coveting. Psalms 73:3-11 says, "For I envied the arrogant when I saw the prosperity of the wicked. They have no struggles; their bodies are healthy and strong. They are free from common human burdens; they are not plagued by human ills. Therefore pride is their necklace; they clothe themselves with violence. From their callous hearts comes iniquity; their evil imaginations have no limits. They scoff, and speak with malice; with arrogance they threaten oppression. Their mouths lay claim to heaven, and their tongues take possession of the earth. Therefore their people turn to them and drink up waters in abundance. They say, 'How would God know? Does the Most High know anything?'" There is an answer for that in Proverbs 23:17-18, which states, "Do not let your heart envy sinners, but always be zealous for the fear of the Lord. There is surely a future hope for you, and your hope will not be cut off." While coveting usually involves tangible objects, we tend to envy intangibles that often turn out to be far from what we perceive them to be. In some respects, envy is more dangerous than coveting because if we gain what we envy, for example break up a marriage and marry the spouse, the reality we discover is often a severe disappointment.

Greed is the next creation of a misplaced value system. Greed is prioritizing getting something above what is important in life. Greed is not something that just happens, however. Before you become greedy, you must make something an idol by giving it an inflated place in your life. As with most things, this is a financial principle that applies to everything in life. Your idol may be money, a car, your perception of success, or a person. If you do not recognize and deflate what you have become obsessed with, then your drive to acquire it can become the driving force in your life, and you have reached the point of greed. Job 24:1-3 describes what it looks like in an agrarian society when he says, "There are those who move boundary stones; they pasture flocks they have stolen. They drive away the orphan's donkey and take the widow's ox in pledge. They thrust the needy from the path and force all the poor of the land into hiding."

Ecclesiastes 5:8-12 modernizes it for us when it says, "If you see the poor oppressed in a district, and justice and rights denied, do not be surprised at such things; for one official is eyed by a higher one, and over them both are others higher still. The increase from the land is taken by all; the king himself profits from the fields. Whoever loves money never has enough; whoever loves wealth is never satisfied with their income. This too is meaningless. As goods increase, so do those who consume them. And what benefit are they to the owners except to feast their eyes on them? The sleep of a laborer is sweet, whether they eat little or much, but as for the rich, their abundance permits them no sleep." Some people believe only rich people are greedy, but greed is not affected by your wealth, as Jeremiah 6:13 points out. "From the least to the greatest, all are greedy for gain; prophets and priests alike, all practice deceit." Some of the wealthiest people I know are the most generous, while some who live on welfare constantly complain what they get from the government and local charities is never enough or good enough and are, in reality, the greediest people I know. Greed is always a personal decision to prioritize Stuff and getting that Stuff above God and their family.

On the opposite end of the spectrum of misplaced value is laziness. Not recognizing the value of something is just as dangerous as over-valuing it. When someone values playing video games or reading books or magazines higher than earning money needed for their daily existence, it is a huge problem, especially for those who choose to care for them. When someone values the thrill of betting above caring for themselves, a life of debt and misery is guaranteed. When someone values their next cigarette more than providing for their family, their quality of life and family environment both suffer. Solomon counsels lazy people to take the example of ants in Proverbs 6:6-11, "Go to the ant, you sluggard; consider its ways and be wise! It has no commander, no overseer or ruler, yet it stores its provisions in summer and gathers its food at harvest. How long will you lie there, you sluggard? When will you get up from your sleep? A little sleep, a little slumber, a little folding of the hands to rest—and poverty will come on you like a thief and scarcity like an armed man." Laziness is a hot topic in Proverbs, and another verse is Proverbs 13:4 which says, "A sluggard's appetite is never filled, but the desires of the diligent are fully satisfied." It isn't ignored in the New Testament either, where Hebrews 6:12 says, "We do not want you to become lazy, but to imitate those who through faith and patience inherit what has been promised." As destructive and seductive as laziness is, it is perhaps the easiest to overcome be-cause when a lazy person begins to appropriately value themselves and begins to work, the increased self-esteem and freedom earned from being responsible for themselves usually positively reinforces their be-havior and keeps them motivated to continue their efforts.

While I was in high school a "few" years ago, I was on a Future Prob-lem Solving team. Even though it was a very small school (I graduated in a class of thirteen), two of the other members were delayed hippies and the other was probably a socialist. It made for some interesting and creative solutions, but I value those times and friends highly still. We had at least four competitions that year, and the answer to every competition was to return to an agrarian society. That solution eliminated many transportation issues, overcrowding, gang violence and the concentration of poverty in certain areas. We did very well that year, and the message from then rings true in this area as well. The further we get away from working with our hands to grow our own food, build our own houses, and own responsibility for providing for safe and healthy communities, the more difficult it becomes to correctly value and prioritize our efforts.

The overall concept of value is probably best demonstrated in Luke 14:11-32, commonly known as the ever-versatile story of the Prodigal Son. To summarize the story, there was a successful farmer who had two sons. The younger son had no interest in keeping up the family business. He begged his father for his inheritance early so he could go live it up somewhere else. Eventually his father agreed, which meant he probably had to sell part of his land and livestock. The son took his new-found wealth, moved to another country and rapidly blew everything on wine, women, and song. He eventually ended up trying to survive by feeding pigs, which are forbidden animals for Jews. He comes to his senses and goes back to his father to beg for a servant's job because he knew it would be much better than what he was doing. When he returned, his father restored him as a son and threw a feast for him, which made the older son so angry he refused to participate in it.

How does this story tie into the concept of value? Initially the son was in the position to inherit his portion of the successful family business, even though he got half as much as the older one. If he would have submitted to his father's authority, he would have learned the principles of successful business management. Instead of correctly valuing those things, he chose instead to blow his fortune and guaranteed future for a few months of getting drunk with prostitutes and other priorities of the young wealthy crowd where he lived. By ignoring the values and principles of how he had been raised, he was soon rewarded by being not only completely broke but also unemployable in the trades of the local culture. When hunger and desperation brought him back to appropriately valuing things, he returned to his home, an environment where everything was valued based on God's perspective. When he appropriately valued and prioritized everything in life, he was not only restored to his elevated position, but he also began to restore his wealth status as well. That is a topic we will look at in more detail later.

Money and possessions are temporary things we enjoy along the path of life. When we put God in first place in our lives, we strive to fulfill our life mission of serving God and others with the things God gives us along the way. When we allow ourselves to be distracted by Stuff, we lose our sense and perspective of prosperity and become easily distracted into other sins to try to satisfy our inappropriate desires. The way to achieve prosperity and avoid debt driven by materialism and instant gratification is to stay focused on God and His priorities.

EARN YOUR KEEP

As Christians we are supposed to honor God with our tithes, support our families, and be generous to others. It is impossible to do any of those without having money and other resources ourselves. There is an underlying assumption that you are earning money some way. Most of us must work to earn that money, while others who have saved and invested long enough can use their interest and returns. There is more than an assumption of earning your own way in the Bible, however. There are some verses that clearly say it, and here are a few of them:

> Proverbs 12:11 Those who work their land will have abundant food, but those who chase fantasies have no sense.

> Proverbs 12:14 From the fruit of their lips people are filled with good things, and the work of their hands brings them reward.

> Proverbs 14:23 All hard work brings a profit, but mere talk leads only to poverty.

> Romans 4:4-5 Now to the one who works, wages are not credited as a gift but as an obligation. However, to the one who does not work but trusts God who justifies the ungodly, their faith is credited as righteousness.

> 2 Timothy 2:6 The hardworking farmer should be the first to receive a share of the crops

The message is clear: we are expected to earn our own way as long as we are physically and mentally able. If we were able to choose whether or not to work, most of us would opt to stay at home and pursue our own interests. While that sounds like a good plan to follow, we have a moral responsibility to use our lives to give value back to our families and society as a whole. This is often done by exchanging our time and abilities for money, but a parent staying at home and providing a healthy environment for growing children provides as much value as someone working full time. Either way, the person is creating a better environment for themselves and their families by conscientiously working. Choosing to not work is strongly frowned upon in the Bible.

Proverbs 6:6-11 Go to the ant, you sluggard;

consider its ways and be wise!

It has no commander,

no overseer or ruler,

yet it stores its provisions in summer

and gathers its food at harvest.

How long will you lie there, you sluggard?

When will you get up from your sleep?

A little sleep, a little slumber,

a little folding of the hands to rest—

and poverty will come on you like a thief

and scarcity like an armed man.

Proverbs 10:4-5 Lazy hands make for poverty,

but diligent hands bring wealth.

He who gathers crops in summer is a prudent son,

but he who sleeps during harvest is a disgraceful son.

Proverbs 19:14 Laziness brings on deep sleep,

and the shiftless go hungry.

Ecclesiastes 10:18 Through laziness, the rafters sag;

because of idle hands, the house leaks.

Hebrews 6:12 We do not want you to become lazy, but to imitate those who through faith and patience inherit what has been promised.

2 Thessalonians 3:7-15 For you yourselves know how you ought to follow our example. We were not idle when we were with you, nor did we eat anyone's food without paying for it. On the contrary, we worked night and day, laboring and toiling so that we would not be a burden to any of you. We did this, not because we do not have the right to such help, but in order to offer ourselves as a model for you to imitate. For even when we were with you, we gave you this rule: "The one who is unwilling to work shall not eat." We hear that some among you are idle and disruptive. They are not busy; they are busybodies. Such people we command and urge in the Lord Jesus Christ to settle down and earn the food they eat. And as for you, brothers and sisters, never tire of doing what is good. Take special note of anyone who does not obey our instruction in this letter. Do not associate with them, in order that they may feel ashamed. Yet do not regard them as an enemy, but warn them as you would a fellow believer.

When someone works, there is an expectation of being compensated for it. Compensation varies with the type of work performed. For a stay-at-home mother they are, or should be, compensated by appreciation from their children and spouse for the training and comfortable environment they provide. For those just entering the workforce, it is earning a little as they gain experience. The longer you work and the better you perform your job the more you should earn. Business owners and managers should earn more because of their additional responsibilities. When you work in an economy where you are not assigned a job, it is your responsibility to make changes if you are not happy with what you are earning, either through acquiring additional skills and education or by moving to a different employer or business. In all circumstances, employees should be compensated fairly based on their skills, performance, and the skill level of the job itself. Here are a few verses that support this:

> Genesis 29:15 Laban said to him, "Just because you are a relative of mine, should you work for me for nothing? Tell me what your wages should be."

> Deuteronomy 24:14-15 Do not take advantage of a hired worker who is poor and needy, whether that worker is a fellow Israelite or a foreigner residing in one of your towns. Pay them their wages each day before sunset, because they are poor and are counting on it. Otherwise they may cry to the Lord against you, and you will be guilty of sin.

> Matthew 20:8 "When evening came, the owner of the vineyard said to his foreman, 'Call the workers and pay them their wages, beginning with the last ones hired and going on to the first.'

> Romans 4:4 Now to the one who works, wages are not credited as a gift but as an obligation.

> 1 Timothy 5:18 For Scripture says, "Do not muzzle an ox while it is treading out the grain," and "The worker deserves his wages."

Farmers and ranchers do not earn wages. They put in thousands of hours fighting the land and weather in hopes of harvesting enough to cover their expenses with enough left over to save for a bad year. The same can be said of pastors and full-time parents who put in thousands of hours to improve the lives of their church families and children in hopes they will reap a harvest of improved lives. There are more verses in the Bible about the expectation of harvest since the Israelites spent most of their history in agriculture. Some verses about harvest are included here:

> Ezekiel 34:27-28 The trees will yield their fruit and the ground will yield its crops; the people will be secure in

their land. They will know that I am the Lord, when I break the bars of their yoke and rescue them from the hands of those who enslaved them. They will no longer be plundered by the nations, nor will wild animals devour them. They will live in safety, and no one will make them afraid.

Zechariah 8:12 "The seed will grow well, the vine will yield its fruit, the ground will produce its crops, and the heavens will drop their dew. I will give all these things as an inheritance to the remnant of this people.

Hebrews 6:7-8 Land that drinks in the rain often falling on it and that produces a crop useful to those for whom it is farmed receives the blessing of God. But land that produces thorns and thistles is worthless and is in danger of being cursed. In the end it will be burned.

James 5:7 Be patient, then, brothers and sisters, until the Lord's coming. See how the farmer waits for the land to yield its valuable crop, patiently waiting for the autumn and spring rains.

No matter how we chose to earn a living, we all have a moral responsibility to work unless a professional physician certifies we are unable to for physical or mental reasons. It does not matter if that work involves raising children at home, punching ideas into a computer, performing lab work, or building something. The important thing is you produce something that provides value to your family and community in exchange for compensation. The type of work is not important, but recognizing you play a role in your community and are responsible for it is. That is the reason Jesus said the second most important commandment is to love others as yourself. Part of loving others is caring for their physical needs, and to do that we must have the finances and resources to be able to provide that care.

LOANS

Christians have a love/hate relationship with loans. There are many verses in the Bible telling us we should avoid them. There are more verses saying loans should be fair, just, and repaid, so it is obvious loans were common for centuries. It is important to understand that although loans have become integral for many cultures, the justification for them has changed dramatically over time. It is this change in thinking that has created the financial crisis many people currently experience more than the tool itself.

Loans did not exist in the first cultures. Life was financially simple back then. If you did not have it, you improvised. If you did not have a spear to kill your prey, you used a big rock. If you did not have a scythe to harvest your crop, you used a big knife to cut your grain. If you broke your knife on a rock and did not have time to make a new one before rain wiped out your harvest, you would negotiate with a neighbor to cut your crop in exchange for beating the grain out of his bundles of wheat once they were safely out of the weather. It was either a do-it-yourself chore, or you negotiated with your community to work together and divide the proceeds later. This system had many advantages, including the hostile people surviving on their own and those who could get along forming close relationships as they worked together to provide the basics of life.

Loans aren't mentioned until Exodus, which is after the Israelites and other nations had organized into family clans and some had settled into permanent locations. As they began shifting away from roaming agrarian cultures, some people shifted into specific occupations instead of doing everything for themselves or trading for what they could not produce. This specialization allowed more advanced development of tools and end products. As these specialized products entered circulation, the superior products and limited number available increased demand for using them. As the number of families increased and more land was put in production, the demand for specialized tools increased so it was more feasible to loan the tools between clans instead of clans combining to cooperatively harvest the products.

Personal loans were first mentioned in Exodus 22:25-27, which says, "If you lend money to one of my people among you who is needy, do not treat it like a business deal; charge no interest. If you take your neighbor's cloak as a pledge, return it by sunset, because that cloak is the only covering your neighbor has. What else can they sleep in? When they cry out to me, I will hear, for I am compassionate." The loans were only to cover basic necessities of life and were extremely short term. They were done out of compassion and made without interest. This is essentially the opposite of how loans are used in technologically advanced cultures today.

The concept continued in Leviticus 25:35-38 which reiterates, "If any of your fellow Israelites become poor and are unable to support themselves among you, help them as you would a foreigner and stranger, so they can continue to live among you. Do not take interest or any profit from them, but fear your God, so that they may continue to live among you. You must not lend them money at interest or sell them food at a profit. I am the Lord your God, who brought you out of Egypt to give you the land of Canaan and to be your God." Loans were acts of compassion with the focus strictly on the survival of the borrower without any profit to the lender.

The concept of loans was modified slightly in Deuteronomy 23:19-20 which says, "Do not charge a fellow Israelite interest, whether on money or food or anything else that may earn interest. You may charge a foreigner interest, but not a fellow Israelite, so that the Lord your God may bless you in everything you put your hand to in the land you are entering to possess." This kept in place the ban on lenders earning interest on loans to their own race. However, they were allowed to reasonably profit from lending to other races. This easement set in place the basics for lending money as an occupation, with profit coming from foreigners.

As the business of lending became more common, additional laws were put in place to regulate the practice. Deuteronomy 15 put a time limit on all loans to fellow Israelites at seven years and continued the ban on charging interest to them. This time limit again did not apply to loans made to foreigners, which allowed people to charge higher rates of interest for longer terms. This reinforced the concept of compassion to those around you but increased the potential for profit to those made to other nationalities.

We know loans have been around for a long time. The question we need to ask is if they are something we should use. The short answer is no, or at least only as a last resort. There are several verses that emphasize this, so here are several of them to chew on:

> Deuteronomy 28:44 They will lend to you, but you will not lend to them. They will be the head, but you will be the tail.

> 1 Kings 4:1 The wife of a man from the company of the prophets cried out to Elisha, "Your servant my husband is dead, and you know that he revered the Lord. But now his creditor is coming to take my two boys as his slaves."

> Proverbs 6:1-2 My son, if you have put up security for your neighbor,

> if you have shaken hands in pledge for a stranger,

> you have been trapped by what you said,

> ensnared by the words of your mouth.

> Proverbs 22:7 The rich rule over the poor,

> and the borrower is slave to the lender.

> Proverbs 22:26-27 Do not be one who shakes hands in pledge

> or puts up security for debts;

> if you lack the means to pay,

> your very bed will be snatched from under you.

The consequences of borrowing money are clear. When you borrow money from either a person or a business you give them control over part of your finances until it is paid off. You also give them the ability to seize the property the loan is based on if you fail to pay it off in the time it is written for. Considering your finances and possessions are supposed to be set aside to serve God, allowing someone else to take control of them should be avoided.

How should we reconcile this view with the cold, hard fact that inflation has driven up the price of everything to the point where it takes a large sum of money to purchase things that are necessary in our society, such as housing and transportation? First it is important to realize cultures based on materialism have their priorities backwards, and we should re-evaluate our priorities to keep them in line with God's expectations. Here are some basic areas where a different perspective would be helpful.

Education:

We are taught we must go to college to get a good education so we can get a good job and earn lots of money. As long as this view holds, tuition will continue to outgrow inflation, throwing people deeper into debt for longer periods of time. There are several problems with this approach, however.

- Calling: Not everyone should be a doctor, lawyer, scientist, or business professional. The first step in preparing for a career should be prayer along with aptitude and interest testing. If someone is called to be a minister, they should attend a seminary. If someone is called to be an electrician, they need to attend a trade school. If someone does not feel a specific calling, there is nothing wrong with working their way through the ranks in Wal-Mart, McDonalds, or another business instead of burying themselves in debt for classes they may never use.

- Preparation: There is an alarming movement that children should have a free pass until they become adults, and they should not work until they are older teenagers. This is dangerous for many reasons. First, kids learn most of their money management skills by the time they are seven years old, so if they are not taught the basics by then, their chances of financial success plummet. Second, they cannot develop a successful work ethic if they never work. Third, part of teaching kids financial skills should be making them tithe and set aside at least ten percent for future needs such as cars and higher education. These three areas of preparation are vital for children to learn as they mature to become financially successful as adults.

- Value: Many high school graduates are essentially forced to attend college after they graduate from high school. The problem with this is not only debt, but the value of general education classes they are forced to take has become increasingly questionable. While true education exposes students to a wide variety of ideas and perspectives, many liberal arts courses have reached the level of indoctrination through intimidation and ridicule in subjects such as evolution, feminism, and extremely biased views of history.

- Cost: While the cost per semester hour keeps rising, there are less expensive alternatives available. Community colleges are useful for getting general education requirements out of the way at significantly lower prices. Online courses are even more reasonable. The key to using alternative methods of education is finding ones that are accredited and where credits transfer to your ultimate college or university of choice so you do not end up being forced to retake the same classes.

Transportation:

There are three ways materialism misleads us about transportation. Believing any one of them can be costly, and following all three sucks thousands of dollars out of a family's budget every year. Carefully evaluating how these affect your life can be highly beneficial to your financial success.

- Everyone needs their own vehicle. If you live in an urban area, you do not need a vehicle for every adult in your house with some long-term planning. Utilize public transportation if it is available. Intentionally support businesses close to you so you can walk or ride a bike to them. Coordinate trips so everyone can run their chores at the same time.

- You need to buy a new car. Whenever you purchase a new vehicle, its value decreases by at least 10% as soon as you drive it off the lot. Instead of buying new, get a used one you can pay cash for and "invest" what you would spend on a car payment every month into an emergency fund or savings account to have cash to pay for repairs and eventually replace the vehicle.

- You need a new car every three years. Car companies and banks love this thinking. Car loans used to be written for three years, so as soon as you paid off your car you would walk in and get a loan to buy a new one. Instant predictable demand for dealerships and a reliable source of interest for financial institutions. While new car loans now stretch up to five years, this does not change the turnover rate and actually increases your interest costs since you consistently roll over what you still owe on your old car into the new car loan.

- It is a vehicle, not an ego trip. If you know someone who has to clean their vehicle every time it gets a spot on it, does not allow anyone to eat or drink in it, has to drive slow over bumps to prevent it from bouncing too hard, and has to straddle two parking spots to prevent it from getting scratched, they have a problem with materialism. While it is fine to put time and effort into keeping your vehicle in good mechanical and physical condition, if the vehicle becomes more important than how it is used to serve God and others, there is a serious issue. The same goes for what is in the home and what you wear. Appearances are nothing to God, and we should constantly remind ourselves of that.

Homes:

As people are convinced to spend more and more money on education and vehicles, the amount of income left to pay for a place to live shrinks until it barely covers rent. This leaves less money to save to purchase a home. When combined with the materialistic demand for larger and more sophisticated houses and outrageous prices in urban locations, this eliminates more families from home ownership every year if they chase the Stuff instead of Relationship.

Stuff:

Credit card debt and payroll loans are the most dangerous types of loans. Sometimes that debt comes from medical emergencies and car repairs. Frequently they come from misplaced priorities. Does having a larger TV, new furniture, or going on vacation really fulfill your mission of serving God? New things and relaxation are not wrong, but they should always be taken in the context of avoiding debt.

These four examples will hopefully help you re-evaluate your spending priorities. However, even after reexamining your priorities, sometimes it is still necessary to get a loan for emergencies and large necessary purchases. What are the Biblical rules to follow once we have a loan?

The first rule is to prioritize paying back what you owe. It does not matter if the item was overpriced or the interest charged was unfair, the point is you agreed to the loan terms and are morally bound to repay what you committed to. This is what gives power to the person or business who wrote you the loan. Here are some verses which confirm this.

> Deuteronomy 28:44 They will lend to you, but you will not lend to them. They will be the head, but you will be the tail.
>
> Psalms 37:21-22 The wicked borrow and do not repay, but the righteous give generously;
>
> Proverbs 22:7 The rich rule over the poor, and the borrower is slave to the lender.
>
> Romans 13:8-10 Let no debt remain outstanding, except the continuing debt to love one another, for whoever loves others has fulfilled the law. The commandments, "You shall not commit adultery," "You shall not murder," "You shall not steal," "You shall not covet," and whatever other command there may be, are summed up in this one command: "Love your neighbor as yourself." Love does no harm to a neighbor. Therefore love is the fulfillment of the law.

There is a major problem with people feeling they do not have to pay back loans. Some think they are entitled to whatever they want and borrow from financial institutions through loans and credit cards until they cannot make the payments, then simply file for bankruptcy and start all over. Some apply for loans with misleading information, then bargain to reduce their balances and get lower payments without considering the moral implications of forcing someone else to cover their losses. Some just keep buying stuff on credit to keep up with the Joneses and expect others (family, aid agencies, the government, and food banks) to cover their necessities while sending most of their income for payments. All of these not only avoid their responsibility to support themselves but disregard their moral responsibilities to pay their debts.

Perhaps where this has gotten the most out of hand is when people, especially college students, rent places to live. When someone rents a place they sign a rental agreement, which is a legal commitment to live in that place for a set amount of time for a specific amount of money. If it is a one-year lease for $750 dollars a month, they are legally committed to pay the owner $9,000.00. There are not caveats for that lease. If you choose your roommates poorly, it is unfortunate, but you are still committed to those terms. If you drop out of school, then great, you have more time to work to pay your lease. If your boyfriend dumps you for your roommate (happens a lot), then it is time to rearrange your schedule and spend more time at the library when they are together, but it isn't a get-out-of-the-lease card. It works the same way with a car loan or lease: if you wreck it the first month you have it, you are still responsible for the payments and paying your insurance deductible. This is why it is important for parents to prepare their children as they grow up so they understand the commitments and responsibilities of entering into financial agreements before they get into trouble with them.

The second rule to follow with loans applies to the lender. They are repeatedly warned against charging too much interest. This still applies to us today, especially since those with the worst credit scores are charged the highest interest rates because of their risk factors. When banks and credit card companies reject their credit requests, they may go to questionable sources for money and those sources charge much higher interest rates. Some verses warning against charging high interest rates (called usury) include:

> Proverbs 28:8 Whoever increases wealth by taking interest or profit from the poor amasses it for another, who will be kind to the poor.

Ezekiel 22:12 In you are people who accept bribes to shed blood; you take interest and make a profit from the poor. You extort unjust gain from your neighbors. And you have forgotten me, declares the Sovereign Lord.

Credit unions and banks are the most regulated and safest places to get loans. Credit cards typically have interest rates that qualify as usury unless your credit score is above seven hundred. Insurance companies typically have acceptable interest rates when you borrow money, but you often must have to have a policy with them to qualify. Sources you must avoid borrowing from include pawn shops, payday loans and loan sharks.

The third rule to follow for loans is to never cosign one. While it might seem tempting to "help" someone by saying you trust them to pay for it, the reality is you are putting your finances at risk. When you cosign a loan you agree to take full responsibility for all the payments left if the other person dies, loses their job, or just takes off in the middle of the night. If you have enough savings and investments to cover someone else's loan, then it is your choice to take that risk. If you cannot afford to pay off the loan, then you have a moral responsibility to yourself and your family to say no. What you may not realize is you are enabling someone's poor financial habits by not making them learn how to fix their own financial issues. Verses which tell us to avoid cosigning loans include these.

Proverbs 11:15 Whoever puts up security for a stranger will surely suffer,

but whoever refuses to shake hands in pledge is safe.

Proverbs 17:18 One who has no sense shakes hands in pledge

and puts up security for a neighbor.

Proverbs 22:26-27 Do not be one who shakes hands in pledge

or puts up security for debts;

if you lack the means to pay,

your very bed will be snatched from under you.

The rules so far are fairly predictable. You have heard them if you have gone through any financial training. There is one that is not talked about often, though. With all the warnings against getting a loan, there is a twist. While we are to avoid taking a loan, we are encouraged to be generous in giving loans to others in need. Verses which tell us this include:

> Leviticus 25:35-38 "If any of your fellow Israelites become poor and are unable to support themselves among you, help them as you would a foreigner and stranger, so they can continue to live among you. Do not take interest or any profit from them, but fear your God, so that they may continue to live among you. You must not lend them money at interest or sell them food at a profit. I am the Lord your God, who brought you out of Egypt to give you the land of Canaan and to be your God.

> Deuteronomy 28:12 The Lord will open the heavens, the storehouse of his bounty, to send rain on your land in season and to bless all the work of your hands. You will lend to many nations but will borrow from none.

> Matthew 5:42 Give to the one who asks you, and do not turn away from the one who wants to borrow from you.

> Luke 6:34-35 And if you lend to those from whom you expect repayment, what credit is that to you? Even sinners lend to sinners, expecting to be repaid in full. But love your enemies, do good to them, and lend to them without expecting to get anything back. Then your reward will be great, and you will be children of the Most High, because he is kind to the ungrateful and wicked.

Loans have been around for centuries. They started with borrowing for necessities, but as technology evolved and people became more isolated from their family groups, they have increasingly been used for wants and impulse buys. Taking the time to examine how necessary purchases are and how they align with fulfilling God's mission for you, helps you make wiser decisions on how you commit your future income. When loans become necessary it is important to insure the loans are fair, and you are able to pay them off without interfering with the necessities of life. Following these guidelines can reduce the demands on your current and future income and allow you to be more generous now while building a secure future.

THEFT

It feels a little strange to include a chapter about theft when writing about the theological side of money management, but it is mentioned several times in the Bible, so here we go. It even made the top ten list of sins in Deuteronomy 5:19 when God etched on the stone tablets, "You shall not steal." The more I debated including this chapter, the more I realized the American culture has accepted and excused theft as an acceptable business practice from both the employer and employee. It is active in the church as well, which opened the door into our culture as a whole. Perhaps by addressing this issue it will be easier to get a clear perspective on our overall view of financial management and what steps need to be taken to realign it with God's view.

We start with stealing from God. This is mentioned in several places, but explained well in Malachi 3:8-12 "'Will a mere mortal rob God? Yet you rob me. But you ask, "How are we robbing you?" In tithes and offerings. You are under a curse—your whole nation—because you are robbing me. Bring the whole tithe into the storehouse, that there may be food in my house. Test me in this,' says the Lord Almighty, 'and see if I will not throw open the floodgates of heaven and pour out so much blessing that there will not be room enough to store it. I will prevent pests from devouring your crops, and the vines in your fields will not drop their fruit before it is ripe,' says the Lord Almighty. 'Then all the nations will call you blessed, for yours will be a delightful land,' says the Lord Almighty." By not showing your appreciation to God for providing everything, you steal the blessing of prosperity not only from yourself but your family and the nation as well.

We also steal from God by not caring for our families, the poor, orphans, and widows. One verse that mentions this is Ezekiel 22:29 which says, "The people of the land practice extortion and commit robbery; they oppress the poor and needy and mistreat the foreigner, denying them justice." While it is easy to shift the responsibility for the least fortunate onto the government, that does not erase the moral responsibility we have for their care. It is easy to disown responsibility for the poor to the government, but it is also obvious in our culture of divorce and moving the elderly into nursing homes and failing to support them either financially or with personal involvement. Proverbs 19:26 says, "Whoever robs their father and drives out their mother is a child who brings shame and disgrace." Failing to take responsibility for those God says we are to care for is another way we rob God.

There is a third way we rob God. Sometimes God gives us instructions on how to do things. When we do them but modify the instructions, we are robbing God of our obedience, which penalizes the reward we are to receive. This frequently occurred with the Israelites when they were sent to war. In Joshua 6 the Israelites were told to destroy the city of Jericho and dedicate all of the wealth to God, but some chose to disregard those instructions. Joshua 7:11-12 tells the story of their disobedience when it says, "Israel has sinned; they have violated my covenant, which I commanded them to keep. They have taken some of the devoted things; they have stolen, they have lied, they have put them with their own possessions. That is why the Israelites cannot stand against their enemies; they turn their backs and run because they have been made liable to destruction. I will not be with you anymore unless you destroy whatever among you is devoted to destruction." Sometimes God chooses a person or group to eliminate a problem. If we decide we need to benefit from that task instead of just doing it as we are asked, our disobedience damages our lives more than the blessing we would have received for doing it the right way would have benefitted us.

There are many ways we are warned about when we do business with other people as well. Since most of these are self-explanatory, I will list some for your consideration here:

> Psalms 62:10 Do not trust in extortion
>
> or put vain hope in stolen goods;
>
> though your riches increase,
>
> do not set your heart on them.
>
> Proverbs 6:30-31 People do not despise a thief if he steals

to satisfy his hunger when he is starving.

Yet if he is caught, he must pay sevenfold,

    though it costs him all the wealth of his house.

Proverbs 13:11 Dishonest money dwindles away,

    but whoever gathers money little by little makes it grow.

Proverbs 20:10 Differing weights and differing measures—

    the Lord detests them both.

Isaiah 10:1-4 Woe to those who make unjust laws,

    to those who issue oppressive decrees,

to deprive the poor of their rights

    and withhold justice from the oppressed of my people,

making widows their prey

    and robbing the fatherless.

What will you do on the day of reckoning,

    when disaster comes from afar?

To whom will you run for help?

    Where will you leave your riches?

Nothing will remain but to cringe among the captives

    or fall among the slain.

Yet for all this, his anger is not turned away,

    his hand is still upraised.

Ezekiel 18:12-13 He oppresses the poor and needy.

He commits robbery.

He does not return what he took in pledge.

He looks to the idols.

He does detestable things.

He lends at interest and takes a profit.

Ezekiel 22:29 The people of the land practice extortion and commit robbery; they oppress the poor and needy and mistreat the foreigner, denying them justice.

Ezekiel 28:18 By your many sins and dishonest trade

you have desecrated your sanctuaries.

So I made a fire come out from you,

and it consumed you,

and I reduced you to ashes on the ground

in the sight of all who were watching.

Mark 11:15-17 On reaching Jerusalem, Jesus entered the temple courts and began driving out those who were buying and selling there. He overturned the tables of the money changers and the benches of those selling doves and would not allow anyone to carry merchandise through the temple courts. And as he taught them, he said, "Is it not written: 'My house will be called a house of prayer for all nations'? But you have made it 'a den of robbers.'"

While there are three basic ways we steal from God, there are many ways we steal from each other. They range from stealing directly through elevated prices or charging excess interest to indirect ways, including leaving early from work and not fulfilling commitments. It may seem like it is okay because everyone else is doing it, but we have a moral responsibility to be honest. Theft is a slippery slope in that if you begin excusing stealing pens or printer paper from your employer, it opens a door that makes it easier to begin stealing another "little thing" in another area of life until it becomes a pattern. This is not an issue of acting like everyone else; it reflects our relationship with God. We see this in Matthew 15:16-20 which says, "'Are you still so dull?' Jesus asked them. 'Don't you see that whatever enters the mouth goes into the stomach and then out of the body? But the things that come out of a person's mouth come from the heart, and these defile them. For out of the heart come evil thoughts—murder, adultery, sexual immorality, theft, false testimony, slander. These are what defile a person; but eating with unwashed hands does not defile them.'" The key to correcting an issue of theft is not justifying it based on the corrupt society we live in but by correcting the relationship with God to address and eliminate the problem.

Theft is not just an issue found as we interact with society. Romans 2:17-24 reminds us of this when it says, "if you are convinced that you are a guide for the blind, a light for those who are in the dark, an instructor of the foolish, a teacher of little children, because you have in the law the embodiment of knowledge and truth—you, then, who teach others, do you not teach yourself? You who preach against stealing, do you steal? You who say that people should not commit adultery, do you commit adultery? You who abhor idols, do you rob temples? You who boast in the law, do you dishonor God by breaking the law? As it is written: 'God's name is blasphemed among the Gentiles because of you.'" Churches are just as susceptible to practicing theft as businesses, and for similar excuses. If a church is led to pay ten percent (a tithe) to either their denomination or missions, when finances are tight that is a tempting area to shortchange until more money comes in. If things are tight, especially in smaller churches, it is easy to excuse shortchanging the pastor's salary until the utilities are caught up. Many churches choose to be less than transparent with their finances so they can shift money around to cover fires so they can avoid taking an honest look at their priorities. Transparency in church finances at all levels is necessary to ensure serving God and the community maintains the top priorities and to prevent personalities from distracting from them.

If theft has become an issue in your life, how should you handle it? There are two steps you must take to eliminate the problem. You not only have to stop committing the sin, but you must make restitution for the theft you have already committed. Neither part is easy, but both are necessary to not just stop building up the penalties of the sin committed but to admit responsibility and make restitution so God may restore your prosperity.

The first step, in the memorable words of Nancy Reagan, is "Just Say No." Stop doing it. The scriptural version is found in Ephesians 4:28 which says, "Anyone who has been stealing must steal no longer, but must work, doing something useful with their own hands, that they may have something to share with those in need." Buy your own pens. Print your personal items at home or take them to an office store who will do them for you. Show up for the full time you are assigned to work. If you work construction, finish all parts of the job and clean everything up when you leave. If you promise to clean the garage, do it when you say you will. It is impossible to describe how to do every job and responsibility here, but these should give you enough to get the idea. When you stop your theft habit, you stop earning more condemnation for your sin, but it does not erase what you have already done.

The second step is asking forgiveness from God and whoever you stole from, and then making restitution for that theft. Numbers 5:5-10 tells us, "The Lord said to Moses, 'Say to the Israelites: "Any man or woman who wrongs another in any way and so is unfaithful to the Lord is guilty and must confess the sin they have committed. They must make full restitution for the wrong they have done, add a fifth of the value to it and give it all to the person they have wronged. But if that person has no close relative to whom restitution can be made for the wrong, the restitution belongs to the Lord and must be given to the priest, along with the ram with which atonement is made for the wrongdoer. All the sacred contributions the Israelites bring to a priest will belong to him. Sacred things belong to their owners, but what they give to the priest will belong to the priest."'" If you shoplifted something in the past, pay back the store with interest. If you walked out on a lease, pay the landlord what you owe them. If you promised to pay a bill and did not follow through, repay the person you stiffed. When you restore your relationship with God, He will lead you sometimes decades into the past about issues. The only way to break the penalties you are experiencing now because of your previous theft is to follow through on every issue He brings to mind so your prosperity can be restored.

LEGACY

As I get older, the one thing that weighs heaviest on my mind is the concept of legacy. This topic is much broader than finances, of course. What will people remember about you when you are gone? Were you honest, caring, compassionate and generous? Were you bitter, insensitive and miserly? Were you most people's nightmare, someone who was so bland and average few people even noticed? If you died today, would your family be able to continue living where they are now and doing what they have been doing, or would they be forced to move and depend on government assistance to survive? All these questions should be considered at least once a year to ensure you are on the right track on all levels of life.

From a financial perspective, many in modern cultures fail to think about leaving a legacy until it is too late. They spend money as soon as they get it and focus on toys and entertainment when they are young, then cram as much into retirement programs at the last minute to provide a minimal lifestyle when they retire. The prevailing attitude is you cannot take it with you when you die, so spend freely and try to use it up. If you use it up early, the government will take care of you, so no problem. Everyone for themselves is another way to put it.

The problem with that attitude is it is directly opposed to the Biblical teachings on legacy. While living you must focus on managing your money well, not only for your future but for your family and community. The goal of Biblical money management is to not only provide for yourself and others well during life but leave financial sustenance for more than one generation of your heirs. This demands not only wise financial management from the beginning of your lives, but wise financial planning as well. Randomly made plans based on the latest financial craze or the most recent popular author is a sure way to not succeed in reaching your long-term financial goals. The only way to reach prosperity is to follow God's plan for money.

If you look through the Bible and focus on the topic of money and possessions, you will find the category with the most verses is inheritance. The first part of the Old Testament is a story of the nation of Israel being promised an inheritance and them fighting to gain control over the territory when they reached the Promised Land. It didn't start with a nation, however. The first time God promised the nation of Israel a vast inheritance was in Genesis 15:1-3 when he told a childless Abram, "After this, the word of the Lord came to Abram in a vision. 'Do not be afraid, Abram. I am your shield, your very great reward.' But Abram said, 'Sovereign Lord, what can you give me since I remain childless, and the one who will inherit my estate is Eliezer of Damascus?' And Abram said, 'You have given me no children; so a servant in my household will be my heir.'" Abram and Sarai were too old to have children when God gave him the promise of lots of children and a major inheritance, so it was not surprising when Sarai laughed when she heard the angel tell Abram the promise.

The promise of inheritance followed the family after Abram and Sarai, now called Abraham and Sarah, had a child that grew up and started having children of his own. Genesis 48:3-4 reminds of this when, "Jacob said to Joseph, 'God Almighty appeared to me at Luz in the land of Canaan, and there he blessed me and said to me, "I am going to make you fruitful and increase your numbers. I will make you a community of peoples, and I will give this land as an everlasting possession to your descendants after you."'" Abraham's descendants kept growing, through their move to Egypt and the slavery that followed, until Moses triggered the plagues and led them through the Nile River to freedom. As they began their journey to the land Abraham came from, God promised every one of them would receive an inheritance of land except the Tribe of Levi who were priests. Numbers 26:52-56 states this when it says, "The Lord said to Moses, 'The land is to be allotted to them as an inheritance based on the number of names. To a larger group give a larger inheritance, and to a smaller group a smaller one; each is to receive its inheritance according to the number of those listed. Be sure that the land is distributed by lot. What each group inherits will be according to the names for its ancestral tribe. Each inheritance is to be distributed by lot among the larger and smaller groups.'" By the time they finished wandering in the wilderness, every leader of every tribe knew exactly where their home would be when they crossed the Jordan River. Once they reached the promised land, the next few years were consumed by each tribe conquering the land they were promised as described in the book of Joshua.

The theme of the nation of Israel being an inheritance continues throughout the Old Testament. Samuel called them this when he anointed Saul to be king in 1 Samuel 10:1, "Then Samuel took a flask of olive oil and poured it on Saul's head and kissed him, saying, "Has not the Lord anointed you ruler over his inheritance?"

The concept of inheritance does not just define Israel, however. Throughout the wars in the Promised Land, as each tribe won their land it was divided by families for their permanent homes. Not only was the land given to them at that time, there was a system where the nearest relative could buy the land if a family did not have any more male heirs as shown in Ruth 4. Even if a piece of land was sold to another family it could be restored to the family during the Year of Jubilee, which was established in Leviticus 25:13, "'In this Year of Jubilee everyone is to return to their own property." Each family was meant to keep the land they were given by God forever, and strict records were kept so that even in times of war, when many were taken to foreign lands, ownership could be reestablished when they returned in the future.

With so much attention on Israel being God's inheritance and passing the land through generations, some may be distracted into believing the focus should just be on providing for your heirs. That is not the case. The New Testament focuses more on building a legacy while you are alive instead of providing for your family when you are gone. There are many aspects of this we should consider.

Matthew 25:34-36 is a favorite sermon topic which says, "Then the King will say to those on his right, 'Come, you who are blessed by my Father; take your inheritance, the kingdom prepared for you since the creation of the world. For I was hungry and you gave me something to eat, I was thirsty and you gave me something to drink, I was a stranger and you invited me in, I needed clothes and you clothed me, I was sick and you looked after me, I was in prison and you came to visit me.'" It emphasizes that you build your legacy every day by how you treat others. If you have a materialistic focus and spend your resources on Stuff while neglecting those around you, you earn your rewards here on earth, and that will be the end of it. If you are compassionate towards those around you as you work towards your goals, you will build a heavenly inheritance with eternal value while you enjoy your earthly rewards for living wisely.

In Luke 12:13-15 we find Jesus confronted with a question of family inheritance. It says, "Someone in the crowd said to him, 'Teacher, tell my brother to divide the inheritance with me.'

Jesus replied, 'Man, who appointed me a judge or an arbiter between you?' Then he said to them, 'Watch out! Be on your guard against all kinds of greed; life does not consist in an abundance of possessions.'" Every year we hear stories of families being torn apart after the death of their parents because they are not happy with their inheritance. Having a will in place that clearly defines how an estate is to be divided will ease this situation. Unfortunately, there will always be people who do not value the gifts they are given and covet what a sibling gets or feel they are entitled to more than they receive. The main message here is stuff really does not matter in the long run, especially when putting the pursuit of it above the value of relationships destroys the family the inheritance is meant to sustain.

It is the parents' responsibility to build a legacy. This is covered in the chapter on Family. It is not a one-sided responsibility, however. Proverbs 11:29 gives the other side of the coin when it says, "Whoever brings ruin on their family will inherit only wind, and the fool will be servant to the wise." One lesson of the Prodigal Son is found in Proverbs 18:21 when it says, "An inheritance claimed too soon will not be blessed at the end." It is true the parents are responsible for creating an inheritance, but the heirs have a responsibility to use the inheritance wisely. A huge part of this responsibility is thrown back onto the parents, whose job it is to teach sound financial management and planning techniques regardless of how they were raised. Financial management courses are easy to find, both inside and outside of the church. I recommend parents and children take at least two courses from different people to get a well-rounded understanding of those principles without being biased by the ideologies of the presenters.

Paul talks about his legacy in Acts 20:32-35 when he says, "Now I commit you to God and to the word of his grace, which can build you up and give you an inheritance among all those who are sanctified. I have not coveted anyone's silver or gold or clothing. You yourselves know that these hands of mine have supplied my own needs and the needs of my companions.

In everything I did, I showed you that by this kind of hard work we must help the weak, remembering the words the Lord Jesus himself said: 'It is more blessed to give than to receive.'" His goal was to develop two different legacies at the same time. His first legacy was self-sufficiency and independence by working a career to fund his efforts as an evangelist. This prevented anyone demanding biased teachings because of a financial hold over him, a lesson many in the ministry should take to heart. The second legacy he created was generosity to those in need with his earnings. This is key in that he personally supported the fundraising causes he championed for churches in need. It is easy for ministers to stand in the pulpit and try to raise money for a variety of causes. That becomes a distracting routine in some churches, but those causes gain another level of interest when the person asking for funds personally supports them.

This ties into a somewhat touchy subject. I see fundraising requests for people wanting to go on missionary trips at least once a month. Missionary trips are wonderful opportunities to serve others and experience different cultures. The problem with many of those trips are the attendee's expectation for other people to pay for them. I understand mission trips are expensive and overseas ones especially so. The issue with fundraising was pointed out to me by the head of an agriculture mission and frequent target of fundraising requests and is the sense of entitlement and lack of committing personal resources many of them have. His rule of thumb was a person raising money for a short-term trip would have to pay at least twenty percent of the cost before he would consider donating to their cause. Committing time is important for these trips, but if someone does not consider them important enough to work to cover at least part of the cost themselves, you must wonder if their desire is more on having fun than supporting the cause itself. There are always ways to raise money, and it should be from sources outside of a person's parents. Children can mow lawns, clean houses, paint, landscape, bake cookies, and rake leaves with minimal supervision. They can organize car washes, egg begs, and numerous other group activities as well. This is a great opportunity for them to learn responsibility and financial management as they become more involved in the process of earning and raising money for these trips.

The legacy of a Christian character is found in Ephesians 5:3-7 which says, "But among you there must not be even a hint of sexual immorality, or of any kind of impurity, or of greed, because these are improper for

God's holy people. Nor should there be obscenity, foolish talk or coarse joking, which are out of place, but rather thanksgiving. For of this you can be sure: No immoral, impure or greedy person—such a person is an idolater—has any inheritance in the kingdom of Christ and of God. Let no one deceive you with empty words, for because of such things God's wrath comes on those who are disobedient. Therefore do not be partners with them." I almost said good character instead of legacy, but there are many people who put on a good front for some people over the years but have the exact opposite character with everyone else. The problem with living a double life is your opposite life will catch up to you eventually, whether through work or social occasions or in a marriage where one day your spouse wakes up with the wrong character on and life is changed forever. There are several verses in the Bible that talk about only having a Godly character, so it does not matter where you are or who you are with, you are the same person. This eliminates years of deceit and webs of lies someone with multiple characters must create to maintain their duplicity, which is exhausting and creates many mental disorders that need professional treatment. Having an honest, consistent character focused on God makes building a Christian legacy a natural part of everyday life.

PLANNING AHEAD

There is an adage the average person spends more time planning what they will eat in a week than planning their retirement in a year. For many families in the United States that is true. On the other hand, there are many who obsess over their investments, switching funds and vehicles every week if not daily. Which ones are most successful when they retire? The real answer is neither one: those who pay the least attention take recommendations that frequently have high fees benefitting their broker, and those who trade all the time eat up their principal paying trading fees. Those who earn the most in their savings and investments get wise advice on where to put their money before setting up the account and check it once or twice a year to make sure it is still performing as predicted, moving it only when there is a significant change in outcome.

From a religious standpoint there are also two extremes. On one side is people who pray about what to wear every day but believe they should just trust God for the future which, in their perspective, means putting minimal effort into planning ahead or investing. On the other side you have people who believe God is not really interested in their day to day activities and take full responsibility for ensuring their future. True success is once again found somewhere in the middle. We must recognize God takes an active interest in all areas of our lives and put Him first, but also educate ourselves and utilize expert advice to use the most efficient methods to achieve our goals.

The main question for this chapter is if it is scriptural to plan for the future or are we supposed to go with the flow and trust God to provide for our needs as they come. I know some who took that approach, and as they grew older frequently requested prayer for money to fix their car or roof or water heater because Social Security and their retirement plans simply did not provide for more than the necessities. By buying into the fear of potentially accumulating too much, they fell into the worse reality of consistently not having enough. On the other hand, those who focus too much on getting more sometimes allow their focus to get pulled away from God onto things that do not matter. Those who have more at the end of their life not only have the independence to enjoy what they have, but they also the ability to fund causes and create businesses that positively affect others.

There are many benefits to planning. The question some Christians have is if it is a Biblical thing to do. The answer is yes. Here are some of the verses that talk about planning for the future. The general message is they recommend it, but some also caution against doing it for the wrong reasons such as having more stuff or becoming lazy:

Proverbs 10:4-5 Lazy hands make for poverty,

but diligent hands bring wealth.

He who gathers crops in summer is a prudent son,

but he who sleeps during harvest is a disgraceful son.

Ecclesiastes 3:4-9 I undertook great projects: I built houses for myself and planted vineyards. I made gardens and parks and planted all kinds of fruit trees in them. I made reservoirs to water groves of flourishing trees. I bought male and female slaves and had other slaves who were born in my house. I also owned more herds and flocks than anyone in Jerusalem before me. I amassed silver and gold for myself, and the treasure of kings and provinces. I acquired male and female singers, and a harem as well— the delights of a man's heart. I became greater by far than anyone in Jerusalem before me. In all this my wisdom stayed with me.

Ecclesiastes 3:1-8 There is a time for everything,

and a season for every activity under the heavens:

a time to be born and a time to die,

a time to plant and a time to uproot,

a time to kill and a time to heal,

   a time to tear down and a time to build,

a time to weep and a time to laugh,

   a time to mourn and a time to dance,

a time to scatter stones and a time to gather them,

   a time to embrace and a time to refrain from embracing,

a time to search and a time to give up,

   a time to keep and a time to throw away,

a time to tear and a time to mend,

   a time to be silent and a time to speak,

a time to love and a time to hate,

   a time for war and a time for peace.

Ecclesiastes 11:1-2 Ship your grain across the sea;

   after many days you may receive a return.

Invest in seven ventures, yes, in eight;

   you do not know what disaster may come upon the land.

1 Chronicles 28:2 King David rose to his feet and said: "Listen to me, my fellow Israelites, my people. I had it in my heart to build a house as a place of rest for the ark of the covenant of the Lord, for the footstool of our God, and I made plans to build it.

Proverbs 12:5 The plans of the righteous are just, but the advice of the wicked is deceitful.

These verses show planning ahead is a good strategy. In fact, it is necessary for someone trying to reach a goal in the future, even if it is not financial. If someone were to run a marathon, they would develop a plan of exercise starting with walking a few blocks until they build up the stamina to run a longer distance than a marathon so they can finish well. Someone planning to build a new house would be wise to plan to reach the financial goal of at least ten percent above the projected cost so they can cover the overruns that inevitably occur. Someone planning to retire must utilize a financial professional who can incorporate the cost of living, housing, medical expenses, and desired activities to calculate a realistic goal and develop a strategy to exceed that goal to cover unexpected expenses along the way.

Those who believe we should just go with the flow and leave the future entirely in God's hands are quick to point to Matthew 6:19-21 "Do not store up for yourselves treasures on earth, where moths and vermin destroy, and where thieves break in and steal. But store up for yourselves treasures in heaven, where moths and vermin do not destroy, and where thieves do not break in and steal. For where your treasure is, there your heart will be also." This is not a warning against planning ahead and accumulating wealth for the future. It is a warning against materialism or making the pursuit and value of that wealth more important than your relationship with God. If your heart and values are right, God will allow you to become prosperous, which includes being able to care for yourself until you die. Wealth can and does disappear in a heartbeat, but a right relationship with God creates a hedge of protection around that wealth.

It seems to be especially popular right now to refuse to seek knowledge and education from those experienced in anything and just go on your own knowledge. When (not if) you mess up, then you learn from personal experience and try something else. If those who believe in this approach had any clue as to how much time and money this costs—that they would save from humbling themselves enough to learn from others—they would abandon that line of thought instantly. There are many verses which talk about this, but Proverbs 15:22 sums it up nicely when it says, "Plans fail for lack of counsel, but with many advisers they succeed." When you are planning something—your retirement, building a house, creating a business, having a successful marriage—the question is not if you should consult with an expert about the best way to do it. The question is if you have talked to enough experts so that you have been able to discover the basic fundamentals for success with your venture while being able to filter out the personal biases of who you are talking to. A good number of experts to talk to before starting something is three, which includes getting three quotes from different contractors, financial and insurance institutions, and marriage experts before selecting the one best fitted for your personal or business needs.

If you do consult a financial professional, the amount you will realistically need to retire will probably shock you. The reality is anyone who retires after 2000 needs over a million dollars in savings and investments to maintain their lifestyles. That number increases by the average rate of inflation which is currently five percent every year. Considering Social Security is on the verge of bankruptcy and more people are drawing out money than contributing to the fund, that is no longer a reliable income source even at the current meager payout rate. Is there a scriptural method to follow to reach our projected retirement needs? To answer that question let us look at the following parable.

> Matthew 25:14-30 "Again, it will be like a man going on a journey, who called his servants and entrusted his wealth to them. To one he gave five bags of gold, to another two bags, and to another one bag, each according to his ability. Then he went on his journey. The man who had received five bags of gold went at once and put his money to work and gained five bags more. So also, the one with two bags of gold gained two more. But the man who had received one bag went off, dug a hole in the ground and hid his master's money.

> "After a long time the master of those servants returned and settled accounts with them. The man who had received five bags of gold brought the other five. 'Master,' he said, 'you entrusted me with five bags of gold. See, I have gained five more.'

> "His master replied, 'Well done, good and faithful servant! You have been faithful with a few things; I will put you in charge of many things. Come and share your mas-

ter's happiness!'

"The man with two bags of gold also came. 'Master,' he said, 'you entrusted me with two bags of gold; see, I have gained two more.'

"His master replied, 'Well done, good and faithful servant! You have been faithful with a few things; I will put you in charge of many things. Come and share your master's happiness!'

"Then the man who had received one bag of gold came. 'Master,' he said, 'I knew that you are a hard man, harvesting where you have not sown and gathering where you have not scattered seed. So I was afraid and went out and hid your gold in the ground. See, here is what belongs to you.'

"His master replied, 'You wicked, lazy servant! So you knew that I harvest where I have not sown and gather where I have not scattered seed? Well then, you should have put my money on deposit with the bankers, so that when I returned I would have received it back with interest.

"'So take the bag of gold from him and give it to the one who has ten bags. For whoever has will be given more, and they will have an abundance. Whoever does not have, even what they have will be taken from them. And throw that worthless servant outside, into the darkness, where there will be weeping and gnashing of teeth.'

Even though Jesus spoke this parable centuries before the stock market was invented, it describes the basic principles for successful retirement planning today. Here are the principles it would be wise to follow through on as you plan for your own financial future.

1. Everyone has money to save and invest, no matter what their income level is.

2. Those who have the most money can afford to invest in the riskiest

opportunities which have the potential to give the highest returns. These could be compared to business investments, investments overseas, individual stocks, high-risk bonds, and similar vehicles.

3. Those with moderate amounts of money to invest should utilize less risky opportunities but can still afford some risk. This compares to mutual funds, bonds, life insurance, and other low-risk vehicles.

4. Those with little money to invest should utilize low-risk investments which, unfortunately, have the lowest rates of return such as savings accounts, money market funds, life insurance investments outside of the market, and low-risk bonds.

5. There is no excuse for burying your money in a can or stuffing it under the mattress, which not only can not earn a return but also loses value every year due to inflation.

6. Those who invest wisely will always gain even more, while those who do nothing will lose what they have.

7. It does not matter where the money came from, once it is in your hands it is your responsibility to manage it wisely.

It is important to plan for the future using the knowledge and tools you acquire from experienced financial professionals. The level of risk you take should be based on how much risk you can tolerate, not just your desired result. Even though you should calculate how much money your nest egg should contain, your goal should always be to exceed your expected need to not only cover any unexpected expenses but to also provide an inheritance for your spouse and children.

RETIREMENT

I have been asked on several occasions if retirement is a Biblical concept. That question does not have an obvious answer, but with a lot of reading and burning brain cells, I have an answer for it. It takes some effort to put together, but I believe this is a reasonable justification for not having to work until you die.

The first time I was asked this it kind of threw me. First it seemed the answer varied depending on your culture and its level of technology. If you live in a low-tech culture based on hunting or farming, retirement would not be an option because not killing or growing your food would mean starvation. In a high tech culture where individual effort is rewarded with money that can be exchanged for necessities, retirement is an option because, even though technology enables you to work longer through less physical effort and better health care, you can also use part of your earnings to save and invest to provide a consistent income without daily work.

If you take a closer look at hunter/gatherer cultures, this viewpoint turns out to be flawed. Most of these cultures allow the elders to reduce or stop physically working and spend their time around the home either caring for children or processing the food brought in by others. There is not a set age where this occurs, however, and is based on physical ability. Although diminished capabilities may frustrate the elders, those cultures typically have immense respect for them, so they are valued and maintain their dignity throughout their lives.

Now it is time to examine the Jewish culture. They began as roving tribes who shepherded sheep and goats, following the forage across the desert. As they found more favorable pastures they dug wells, which led some to settle in specific areas. When they reached the Promised Land, some built towns because they had consistent food and easy access to water. When they relocated to Egypt, they continued their farming lifestyle but were eventually forced to live in camps and work as slaves away from the field.

Once they resettled in Israel, they resumed their farming lifestyle but were still able to settle in towns because food was once again easily accessible.

How did the early Israelites handle old age as they chased their flocks and herds across the desert? We have evidence they did not do very well. Genesis 27:1 tells us blindness from working in the sun was common when it says, "When Isaac was old and his eyes were so weak that he could no longer see, he called for Esau his older son and said to him, 'My son.' 'Here I am,' he answered." Genesis 48:10 tells us Israel had the same issue. Disfiguring injuries weren't unusual, due to a wide variety of reasons including being dropped as infants as happened to Mephibosheth in 2 Samuel 4:4. The idea underlies the story of the Prodigal Son in Luke 15 where the older father was near home supervising what happened on his farm when he spotted the younger son returning. If you consider most older men could not see well and had scars from one or more serious injuries stitched up by their wife, their capability to continue working in the field is highly questionable. The culture would be like Native American or African tribes where the youngest generation of a clan did most of the work, the middle generation worked and supervised, and the elders provided wisdom and guidance to the clan. If this does not reflect the basic concept of retirement, I'm not sure what does.

What may surprise you is the average herder or farmer were not the only ones who practiced retirement. Numbers 8:23-26 says, "The Lord said to Moses, 'This applies to the Levites: Men twenty-five years old or more shall come to take part in the work at the tent of meeting, but at the age of fifty, they must retire from their regular service and work no longer. They may assist their brothers in performing their duties at the tent of meeting, but they themselves must not do the work. This, then, is how you are to assign the responsibilities of the Levites.'" God embedded a rule forcing all priests to retire from lead roles when they turned fifty. This is not a popular idea in our culture where dedicated ministers and a shrinking supply of replacements mean many continue to lead churches until they die. On the other hand, it might be useful to consider whether keeping a younger ministry team may help make going to church more attractive to the next generation through more culturally relevant methods and messages.

As part of the culture moved more into farming communities it enabled the establishment of cities. The role of elders continued to be that of owner and manager. Instead of remaining at home most of the time, they transitioned to sitting at the gates of the city where they transacted business and gave advice. Abraham bought the cave to bury Sarah from Ephron the Hittite while he sat at the gates of his city in Genesis 3:10. Joseph's brothers bought food from him in an Egyptian palace in Genesis 47. Boaz bought the land of Naomi's husband from her guardian-redeemer at the gates of their city in Ruth 4. There are more examples, but the idea is clear. The elder men supervised the work done on their land and transacted business at the city gates while the younger generations were out in the field taking care of the daily operations.

It is time to step forward a few hundred years to New Testament times. The size of the cities increased, and trade became an active means of business, with Rome controlling the flow of goods between provinces. The place of business in cities migrated from the gates to marketplaces. Entrepreneurs and traders took over most of the "technological" business. Lydia sold purple cloth in the marketplace of Thyatira in Acts 16:14. In larger cities different trades had their own marketplaces, like the meat market mentioned in 1 Corinthians 10:25-26. The patriarchal system still existed in rural areas but had largely been replaced by entrepreneurs by that time. Like most industrialized nations today, businesspeople supplied the goods and services everyone needed, and the government taxed everyone to pay for projects like building roads and aqueducts.

How does the concept of retirement apply to us today? We live longer with a quality of life that varies significantly depending on how often we can afford to go to the doctor and treat things as they go wrong. If you take a holistic approach to health by eating natural foods and supplements you generally stay healthier and maintain a good quality of life longer than if you depend on drugs and surgeries to keep you going. No matter which approach you take, age eventually gets to you, and it takes longer to do what used to be routine. Exposure to synthetic chemicals, or just elevated levels of natural ones, interferes with natural metabolism and nerve function, which not only slows us down but also decreases our abilities to make valid decisions. Maintaining physical and mental health is difficult in a culture of instant gratification, preservation, and chemically treating symptoms instead of disease prevention.

The truth is very few people will live full lives until they die. Stressors, caused by either disease, emotional crisis, or chemical imbalances will cause most of us to reach a point we will need someone else to help us do tasks essential for living. While some people stubbornly insist on doing everything for themselves, it would be better to retire from not only occupations but doing the personal care tasks they can no longer adequately do well for themselves.

Even though the concept of retirement is Biblical, there are a couple of catches. Both exceptions can be traced back to technology leading to the abandonment of family-based societies. The first catch is, as people age and lose the capacity to do things for themselves, we frequently convince ourselves we as families are too busy to take care of our parents. The second catch is, as the government created and expanded social safety net programs, it has sucked the financial resources people used to give to their own families and local communities to care for those unable to do it for themselves. Taking care of additional family members, especially ones with severe health issues, becomes an overwhelming financial burden on top of a significant time commitment.

THE CONCEPT
OF PROSPERITY

One of the fastest ways to create a consensus in a conservative evangelical church is to condemn the "Prosperity" or "Health and Wealth" Doctrine. One of the fastest ways to create a consensus in a typical progressive non-denominational church is to condemn the "Money Is Evil" doctrine. Both are discussing how to view money, but from opposite ends of the doctrinal spectrum. So which one is right? Both—although it would be difficult to convince either one of them the opposite viewpoint is valid.

You can have success without prosperity. You can have prosperity without financial success. The reason there is an internal war over how to handle finances in the Church is a lack of understanding what the Bible teaches about money and the concept of prosperity in general. The correct understanding of money and how it should be valued was dealt with in a previous chapter. This one is dedicated to the Biblical view of prosperity and how it should be applied to our lives today.

This discussion must begin by defining prosperity. We will use the one furnished by the 1957 Webster College Edition to get a better understanding of how it was used before being modified to reflect modern bias. Note this is not a scriptural definition, since the concept of prosperity is universal and should not be biased by religion. Prosperity is defined as "prosperous condition; good fortune; wealth; success." A better understanding of how it is used in the Bible is the definition of "prosperous; flourishing; successful." To prosper is to succeed and do well which goes far beyond material wealth.

Biblical prosperity fulfills the ultimate meaning of success. Achieving true prosperity means being successful in all areas of life—religion, family, relationships, and finances. Prosperity cannot be achieved without a deep and growing relationship with God, which allows the Holy Spirit to teach you how to develop relationships with family, friends, and business associates to thrive in a well-rounded life. Wealth is a poor metric to measure how successful someone is, because it comes and goes quickly. Revelations 3:17-18 puts it, "You say, 'I am rich; I have acquired wealth and do not need a thing.' But you do not realize that you are wretched, pitiful, poor, blind, and naked. I counsel you to buy from me gold refined in the fire, so you can become rich; and white clothes to wear, so you can cover your shameful nakedness; and salve to put on your eyes, so you can see." Putting God first aligns your understanding and priorities to enable you to become successful in the other aspects of life as well.

We know we can enjoy prosperity by first obeying God in all things, and secondly learning from those who have proven experience in their area of expertise. This applies to all parts of life—finances, businesses, family, real estate, and anything else you can think of. Most people learn about finances from their parents by default, but they are rarely the best examples you can choose. Increasing your knowledge and acting on the new information is always a choice. Here is a short list of how you can learn to be better in any area of life. As always, choose what you put into your mind carefully because "garbage in, garbage out" will harm you no matter how well dressed up it is.

1. Read one chapter in a "self-help" book every day. Start with the area you struggle with the most and rotate topics. Rotate authors as well to get as broad of a perspective as possible.

2. Attend a weekend workshop and seminar once a year. This is a time investment and usually costs money, but the long-term benefits will far outweigh the temporary cost.

3. Be active in a local religious group throughout the year. You will benefit the most if you are involved in one for your own sex, and a couples one if you are married or in a relationship. If your local church does not have its own groups, find one that allows anyone in the community to participate.

4. At least once a quarter participate in a community outreach effort. This can be something organized by your church, or a valued group such as the Lions Club or Kiwanis Club. This will help expand your

horizons by serving others in your community you may never be exposed to otherwise.

It is important to rotate authors and speakers to get as broad of a perspective as possible and stretch your mind instead of simply reinforcing the message you want to hear. If you are married, let your spouse choose a book or seminar for you to attend once a year. Stick with it until the end without making excuses or being hostile about the subject. You must grow to become prosperous, both in your relationship with God but also with your community and in relevant topics of life. God wants each one of us to prosper, and here are several verses that support this claim:

> Deuteronomy 7:12-15 If you pay attention to these laws and are careful to follow them, then the Lord your God will keep his covenant of love with you, as he swore to your ancestors. He will love you and bless you and increase your numbers. He will bless the fruit of your womb, the crops of your land—your grain, new wine and olive oil— the calves of your herds and the lambs of your flocks in the land he swore to your ancestors to give you. You will be blessed more than any other people; none of your men or women will be childless, nor will any of your livestock be without young. The Lord will keep you free from every disease. He will not inflict on you the horrible diseases you knew in Egypt, but he will inflict them on all who hate you.

> Deuteronomy 28:1-14 If you fully obey the Lord your God and carefully follow all his commands I give you today, the Lord your God will set you high above all the nations on earth. All these blessings will come on you and accompany you if you obey the Lord your God:

> You will be blessed in the city and blessed in the country.

> The fruit of your womb will be blessed, and the crops of your land and the young of your livestock—the calves of your herds and the lambs of your flocks.

Your basket and your kneading trough will be blessed.

You will be blessed when you come in and blessed when you go out.

The Lord will grant that the enemies who rise up against you will be defeated before you. They will come at you from one direction but flee from you in seven.

The Lord will send a blessing on your barns and on everything you put your hand to. The Lord your God will bless you in the land he is giving you.

The Lord will establish you as his holy people, as he promised you on oath, if you keep the commands of the Lord your God and walk in obedience to him. Then all the peoples on earth will see that you are called by the name of the Lord, and they will fear you. The Lord will grant you abundant prosperity—in the fruit of your womb, the young of your livestock and the crops of your ground— in the land he swore to your ancestors to give you.

The Lord will open the heavens, the storehouse of his bounty, to send rain on your land in season and to bless all the work of your hands. You will lend to many nations but will borrow from none. The Lord will make you the head, not the tail. If you pay attention to the commands of the Lord your God that I give you this day and carefully follow them, you will always be at the top, never at the bottom. Do not turn aside from any of the commands I give you today, to the right or to the left, following other gods and serving them.

2 Chronicles 1:11-12 God said to Solomon, "Since this is your heart's desire and you have not asked for wealth, possessions or honor, nor for the death of your enemies, and since you have not asked for a long life but for wisdom and knowledge to govern my people over whom I have made you king, therefore wisdom and knowledge will be

given you. And I will also give you wealth, possessions and honor, such as no king who was before you ever had and none after you will have."

Job 1:9-10 "Does Job fear God for nothing?" Satan replied. "Have you not put a hedge around him and his household and everything he has? You have blessed the work of his hands, so that his flocks and herds are spread throughout the land.

Psalms 1:1-3 Blessed is the one

who does not walk in step with the wicked

or stand in the way that sinners take

or sit in the company of mockers,

but whose delight is in the law of the Lord,

and who meditates on his law day and night.

That person is like a tree planted by streams of water,

which yields its fruit in season

and whose leaf does not wither—

whatever they do prospers.

Jeremiah 17:5-8 This is what the Lord says:

"Cursed is the one who trusts in man,

who draws strength from mere flesh

and whose heart turns away from the Lord.

That person will be like a bush in the wastelands;

they will not see prosperity when it comes.

They will dwell in the parched places of the desert,

in a salt land where no one lives.

"But blessed is the one who trusts in the Lord,

whose confidence is in him.

They will be like a tree planted by the water

that sends out its roots by the stream.

It does not fear when heat comes;

its leaves are always green.

It has no worries in a year of drought

and never fails to bear fruit."

Zechariah 1:16-17 "Therefore this is what the Lord says: 'I will return to Jerusalem with mercy, and there my house will be rebuilt. And the measuring line will be stretched out over Jerusalem,' declares the Lord Almighty. "Proclaim further: This is what the Lord Almighty says: 'My towns will again overflow with prosperity, and the Lord will again comfort Zion and choose Jerusalem.'"

There are many more verses along this line, but this is enough for you to understand it is a consistent theme. Perhaps it is easiest to summarize this part of the chapter by quoting many people's favorite verse. Jeremiah 29:11 says it this way, "'For I know the plans I have for you,' declares the Lord, 'plans to prosper you and not to harm you, plans to give you hope and a future.'" God wants each one of us to have a life that is successful in all aspects. What holds most of us back is our lack of fully seeking and following God's will for us.

Sooner or later almost everyone comes to the realization our lives are not as prosperous as we imagined. Sometimes that means having a great marriage with successful kids even though our savings are not as large as hoped for. Some of us have a smaller bank account than we hoped for, with broken families and a relationship with God that needs improvement. Is there a certain point when we should just give up on being prosperous and settle for mediocrity? Never. Not only is God's desire to make us prosperous a reality, He also promises if we finally fix our relationship with Him, the prosperity we have missed out on in the past will be restored to us several times over in the future. Here are several verses that promised this to people throughout the Old and New Testaments.

> Ezekiel 33:14-15 And if I say to a wicked person, 'You will surely die,' but they then turn away from their sin and do what is just and right— if they give back what they took in pledge for a loan, return what they have stolen, follow the decrees that give life, and do no evil—that person will surely live; they will not die.

> Job 8:6 If you are pure and upright, even now he will rouse himself on your behalf and restore you to your prosperous state. Your beginnings will seem humble, so prosperous will your future be.

> Job 42:10-15 After Job had prayed for his friends, the Lord restored his fortunes and gave him twice as much as he had before. All his brothers and sisters and everyone who had known him before came and ate with him in his house. They comforted and consoled him over all the trouble the Lord had brought on him, and each one gave him a piece of silver and a gold ring.

> The Lord blessed the latter part of Job's life more than the former part. He had fourteen thousand sheep, six thousand camels, a thousand yoke of oxen and a thousand donkeys. And he also had seven sons and three daughters. The first daughter he named Jemimah, the second Keziah and the third Keren-Happuch. Nowhere in all the land were there found women as beautiful as Job's daughters, and their father granted them an inheritance along with their brothers.

Jeremiah 32:44 Fields will be bought for silver, and deeds will be signed, sealed and witnessed in the territory of Benjamin, in the villages around Jerusalem, in the towns of Judah and in the towns of the hill country, of the western foothills and of the Negev, because I will restore their fortunes, declares the Lord."

Zechariah 9:12 Return to your fortress, you prisoners of hope; even now I announce that I will restore twice as much to you.

Matthew 19:28-30 Jesus said to them, "Truly I tell you, at the renewal of all things, when the Son of Man sits on his glorious throne, you who have followed me will also sit on twelve thrones, judging the twelve tribes of Israel. And everyone who has left houses or brothers or sisters or father or mother or wife or children or fields for my sake will receive a hundred times as much and will inherit eternal life. But many who are first will be last, and many who are last will be first.

Philippians 3:13-14 Brothers and sisters, I do not consider myself yet to have taken hold of it. But one thing I do: Forgetting what is behind and straining toward what is ahead, I press on toward the goal to win the prize for which God has called me heavenward in Christ Jesus.

Prosperity is success in all areas of life and is not limited to finances. True success lies in placing God first in your life and allowing the Holy Spirit to guide you in putting the rest of your priorities in the right order. This is the only way you can achieve prosperity. Although this does not guarantee financial wealth, a balanced life will bring more success and enjoyment overall than money could ever provide by itself. If you have not committed to following God and finding the life of prosperity He has planned for you, it is not too late to turn control of your entire life over to Him and have the life of success He has planned restored to you for your obedience.

WOMEN AND WEALTH

As in every part of society, the role of women in finances has evolved significantly through the years. Originally, they were excluded from financial decisions in early patriarchal agrarian cultures; in a few years, most of the wealth in the United States will be controlled by women as the Baby Boomers retire and the men die first. We will look at how the role of women in finances changed in the Bible, then look at some cultural issues in what their goals are in our society today.

The first record of women in connection with finances is found in Deuteronomy 21:10-14 which says, "When you go to war against your enemies and the Lord your God delivers them into your hands and you take captives, if you notice among the captives a beautiful woman and are attracted to her, you may take her as your wife. Bring her into your home and have her shave her head, trim her nails and put aside the clothes she was wearing when captured. After she has lived in your house and mourned her father and mother for a full month, then you may go to her and be her husband and she shall be your wife. If you are not pleased with her, let her go wherever she wishes. You must not sell her or treat her as a slave, since you have dishonored her." Frequently when Israel waged war, they destroyed all the males and took women and children as part of the loot. If one caught their eye, they were allowed to marry her after a purification process but were allowed to divorce her if she was difficult on the condition she was to be freed instead of being sold as a slave.

The next two times women are mentioned in connection to finances was creating protections for them. The first instance was to protect their reputations and provide for their livelihood in case a man married her and unfairly treated her. Deuteronomy 2:13-19 says, "If a man takes a wife and, after sleeping with her, dislikes her and slanders her and gives her a bad name, saying, 'I married this woman, but when I approached her, I did not find proof of her virginity,' then the young woman's father and mother shall bring to the town elders at the gate proof that she was a virgin. Her father will say to the elders, 'I gave my daughter in marriage to this man, but he dislikes her. Now he has slandered her and said, "I did not find your daughter to be a virgin." But here is the proof of my daughter's virginity.' Then her parents shall display the cloth before the elders of the town, and the elders shall take the man and punish him. They shall fine him a hundred shekels of silver and give them to the young woman's father, because this man has given an Israelite virgin a bad name. She shall continue to be his wife; he must not divorce her as long as he lives." The second instance is in Deuteronomy 22:28-29 which tells us, "If a man happens to meet a virgin who is not pledged to be married and rapes her and they are discovered, he shall pay her father fifty shekels of silver. He must marry the young woman, for he has violated her. He can never divorce her as long as he lives." In both instances a man tries to ruin a women's reputation, and the punishment for both violations are the same: pay the father money for the crime and being forced to stay married to her for the rest of their lives. Not only are the women's reputations restored, but the man who sins is forced to live with them until death.

Part of the promise of God to the Israelites for obeying his commands was a restoration of families. In several verses God promised women they would be rescued from widowhood and given husbands and children. Psalms 113:7-9 is one place he says this: "He raises the poor from the dust and lifts the needy from the ash heap; he seats them with princes, with the princes of his people. He settles the childless woman in her home as a happy mother of children. Praise the Lord." This was a huge promise since women depended on men for their livelihood, and producing children to carry on the family line was an expected part of their duties in the family.

Although men were the financial leaders of the family, women were responsible for keeping an efficient home. There are several verses singing the praises of women who wisely manage their household finances. There are about as many verses which say women who unwisely manage their households are a detriment to her family. Here are a few of the verses on both sides of the coin.

> Proverbs 6:26 For a prostitute can be had for a loaf of bread,

> but another man's wife preys on your very life.

Proverbs 12:4 A wife of noble character is her husband's crown,

but a disgraceful wife is like decay in his bones.

Proverbs 14:1 The wise woman builds her house,

but with her own hands the foolish one tears hers down.

Proverbs 31

Luke 15:8 "Or suppose a woman has ten silver coins and loses one. Doesn't she light a lamp, sweep the house and search carefully until she finds it?

As nomad clans grew and began to settle down, the role of urban women changed. While those who were married still focused on raising their families, single women began to start home-based businesses to provide for themselves. Successful businesses allowed the women to remain independent and often expanded to train and provide other women with income. By becoming entrepreneurs these women fulfilled the calling of providing for themselves and reduced the demands on local churches as they provided for those who could not do it for themselves. Here are some references about women-owned businesses in the Bible.

2 Kings 4:7 She went and told the man of God, and he said, "Go, sell the oil and pay your debts. You and your sons can live on what is left."

Proverbs 31:24 She makes linen garments and sells them, and supplies the merchants with sashes.

Acts 16:14 One of those listening was a woman from the city of Thyatira named Lydia, a dealer in purple cloth. She was a worshiper of God. The Lord opened her heart to respond to Paul's message.

Just as women in the Bible grew from being considered possessions to managing households to owning businesses, the role of women has continued changing over the years. Women slowly were accepted into the workplace (until they married), then took over many industrial jobs during World War 1 and continued entering other areas of the workforce. The last career areas women have entered are science and financial management. As more women earn or inherit the financial responsibilities of their household, it is important they educate themselves to manage their assets effectively.

There are several reasons women have not entered financial occupations outside of banking. One is sexism, where financial matters were considered too advanced for women to understand. Another is complexity, as each financial company seems determined to create their own terms, so it is difficult for anyone to understand. Time is another factor, as they usually spend more of their time caring for the house and children and often working outside of the home leaves little time to learn the finer details of money management. One that is not discussed much is the pressure to perform above developing relationships, which is their forte. These are some reasons some women are hesitant to enter the financial realm.

There are important reasons women need to be involved with managing money in the household. Perhaps the most important one is the need to have skills and abilities to know how to manage things when responsibility is handed to them. The second reason is related, which is women generally outlive their spouses and the high frequency of divorce. The number of women who choose not to marry at all, or wait until after their careers are established, continues to rise. Another reason they need to be involved is to understand the importance of setting long-term goals and working towards them in terms of retirement and financial security. For these and other reasons it is vital for women to take an active role in the financial management of not only their retirement planning but also all the household issues faced.

Women have different motivations when they manage money. Their focus is generally short-term in caring for immediate needs instead of thinking long-term about funding their own future needs. They generally are focused on relationships and will risk everything for children and close relatives while being conservative with their savings and investments. They are driven more by emotions instead of logic, which can lead to making choices with their heart rather than carefully analyzing the options for those most likely to succeed. These motivations can lead to decisions which seriously harm their own long-term needs, but they do not consider the consequences before impulsively following their hearts.

The financial role of women changed significantly throughout the Bible and continues to change today. It is now more important than ever for women to become involved in financially managing their retirements and homes so they will increase their knowledge and capabilities as they gain control over their family's finances now and in the future.

CAPITALISM OR SOCIALISM

There is an ongoing debate in and about Christianity of the most appropriate economic model to follow. One side points to the emphasis on generosity and the existence of early communal churches as proof that socialism is the best model. The other side points to thousands of years of clans working together and producing goods which are then either traded or sold to purchase goods they cannot make for themselves. The war of words rages, but little has changed as time goes on. I will argue both sides have some good points, but the us versus them context the arguments are frequently framed in are straw men which fall apart when viewed from a Biblical perspective.

Most arguments for socialism are taken out of context and modern strictures placed on them which did not exist in the era they were recorded. When viewed in the age and mindset of the early church, the ideas made sense in the short term. As time went on and the Messiah did not appear, the early church communes fell apart as people were forced to go back to work to support themselves and the indigent they cared for. Remnants of communes continue, not only as monasteries and convents but also as organized communes with pseudo religious convictions which most often fail and are abandoned within a few years.

The reality is the message of the Gospel has nothing to do with an economic system. The Bible is a strictly a religious and historical document focusing on the conduct of individuals as they model their lives on Christ, part of the one true God. While it is true the Bible mentions financial principles many times, and the basic concepts of capitalism are derived from it, anyone who tries to turn it into an economic textbook completely misses the point. If we compare the Bible to the United States political system, the rules and guidelines in it would be comparable to state laws that clarify how to follow the laws set forth in the Constitution and established in the federal system. In an economic system it is (the most important) textbook on how to create and grow a values-based financial lifestyle. While Christians strive to integrate their faith and its concepts into everyday life, using it in any system to try to force certain behaviors or attitudes from those who are not Christians is an effort doomed to failure.

Now that we have discarded the thought of fighting over an economic system, it is time to focus on economic principles people claim to base on Biblical principles and give a hopefully unbiased view of them. The ones already mentioned in detail in other places in the Bible will be discussed, but please refer to those sections for specific verses supporting them.

The entire capitalism-versus-socialism debate is based on two principles found in the Bible. While both principles are valid, understanding the thoughts and reasons behind each are important to see how they do and do not support an economic system. It is also important to understand an economic system by digging into the history of it, such as the lives and writings of those who originated it, before claiming to support it because those espousing either system frequently do not understand anything about it when questioned by an expert in the field.

Capitalism is founded on the principle that everyone who is capable of working is responsible for providing for themselves and their families. People who are innovative and creative produce new and unique products that bring value to others, and those who recognize the value of those products purchase them. The more value a product brings to someone the more they are willing to pay for it. The more people the product brings value to the more units the producer will sell. The producer has incredible flexibility in that they can increase or decrease the price based on availability, or they can choose to barter their good or service for another product instead of selling it. In theory, a person will never be successful unless they produce something, and the value and uniqueness of the product they produce defines how successful they will become.

Some will argue capitalism fails because control of products become concentrated in the hands of a few wealthy people, who control the rest of the economy through manipulation and artificial scarcity. That has happened in the past, but the likelihood of it occurring again is unlikely due to three factors. Each factor is a powerful force, but when they are combined in a free and open society any effort to gain control in any way other than producing better and unique products are quickly sniffed out.

The first factor is the force of the customer, or public opinion. If a farmer traded injured and diseased animals for a large pile of vegetables in ancient Persia, soon he would be forced to only eat meat because word would spread, and nobody would trade for his inferior animals. If Benjamin Franklin had written outrageous lies and slandered his neighbors on his printing press instead of writing funny and thought-provoking essays, he would have gone bankrupt and would never have achieved political fame. If you buy a toilet seat that breaks within a week you would return it to the store, creating an economic loss for them, and warn your neighbors to avoid that product. Now public opinion has a more powerful force called social media, so you can not only warn your friends and neighbors about the inferior toilet seat but warn complete strangers around the globe about the company that produced it. Public opinion is the most powerful force available to ensure goods and products that are inferior or cheap imitations are knocked out of the marketplace before they bring wealth to the producer.

The second factor is government. Government is a double-edged sword in an economy. An open and ethical government will help ensure products offered in the economy are legal (not copycats of someone else's work), safe (made from non-toxic materials), and reasonable (prevent monopolies). In other economies, such as feudalism and socialism, the government slants business towards their friends and either prevents competition or forces people to buy certain products, which drives up prices, increases scarcity, and prevents unbiased economic growth based on bribes or political favors.

I will call the third factor peer pressure for the lack of a better term. This factor strives to increase demand for a product through artificial means. In the professional world it is driven by advertising agencies. In the world of fashion, designers make a tiny alteration in a design then use advertising to blast the message that if you do not have the latest variation you are socially inept. In the social world it is peer pressure created by those who are suckered into the advertising messages then show disdain towards those who do not buy into the message due to either common sense or the economic reality their money has more important uses than to please others.

Socialism is the belief that everyone is entitled to a basic existence. This shows up as universal "free" health care, government subsidies, a "living wage". and minimum retirement income. The basic premise of it is the government is responsible to provide everyone the same level of existence, which is the opposite of the principles taught and modeled in the Bible. This is not only bad for the mental health and well-being of the individual, it violates several basic economic principles as demonstrated in the Soviet Union, Cuba, and Venezuela for specific examples.

There are four basic problems with this economic system. First, the money must come from somewhere, and it is initially taken from the most successful, which decreases the incentive to create new products and wealth. Secondly, there is little incentive for those at the bottom of the economic ladder to produce anything, since they can exist without putting out any effort. Third, those at the lowest economic level are never satisfied with what they have and demand more, which sucks more money from those who succeed and puts more roadblocks into the overall economy. Lastly, the government does not make or create any wealth but can only take it from its citizens, so the political class works to appease the masses who produce little without understanding or being held accountable for the damage they cause to the producers.

In theory, socialism is designed to fulfill one of the basic premises of Christianity, that of compassion. Compassion says everyone should have food to eat. Compassion says everyone should have clothes to wear. Compassion says everyone should have places to live. Compassion says everyone should have access to quality healthcare. Compassion says everyone should have their basic needs taken care of so they can focus on achieving success.

Where the theory of socialism falls apart when it is put into practice is compassion is tied directly to generosity. Anyone can look at someone who lacks what we consider the basics of living and have compassion. Compassion is an emotion, one which many people are eager to show. They start by talking about the person or group that currently has their attention to their friends and relatives. If they hold their attention long enough, they will bring the target to the attention of their church community, perhaps through the sermons or by holding a fundraiser or food drive for them. If the group stays in the limelight long enough, either through local engagement or press attention, there will be organized community meetings about the situation. By the time a handful of community meetings have taken place, a new social issue replaces the last concern and the organizer moves on with the changing limelight. People have met, community engagement achieved with the usual group of social justice advocates, and the effort is declared a success—even though nothing has changed with the group through education, intervention, or laws enacted.

While compassion is a wonderful quality to have, its purpose is to catch your attention about someone or something that needs changed. If it leads to talk and community engagement that is nice, as it is part of the steps needed to make permanent change. If attention to the situation decreases as fast as the number of hits on related news stories, it is obvious the reason for focusing on the issue had more to do with maintaining the reputation of being a social activist than it was about solving the problem. As they say, talk is cheap. In most cases it takes years of blood, sweat, and tears to make significant changes. People who grow up in a culture focused on instant gratification simply do not have the time or dedication to stick with something that long, and it is hard to find people who have explored the process needed to make those changes possible.

Generosity is where the rubber meets the road for social justice. It is not generous to look at a situation and decide someone should take care of it while you are busy maintaining your spot on the bowling team and funding the local Starbucks with your coffee habit. Attending meetings once a month about social justice issues is more about compassion, since you are not actively giving of your resources towards a specific issue until a needed goal is achieved. Going to a spaghetti dinner for someone with serious medical issues is a start towards being generous, but true generosity would be demonstrated by donating money to the family on an ongoing basis and providing transportation, food, or cleaning services for them. While jumping between causes giving a little bit here and there is somewhat generous, true generosity involves choosing one or two causes God puts on your heart and consistently pouring into them until the desired objective is reached, which may take years or decades.

Now that we have chased a rabbit clear through its hole, how does that tie into economics? The theory of socialism is to be generous to everyone. That is a contradiction in terms, because once you force someone through taxes or targeted production goals it is no longer generosity. Generosity by definition is voluntary. Forced contributions through taxation, redistribution, and central planning consistently fail because nobody can accurately predict the future and crop failures, mediocre production efforts, and un-informed/nonscientific methods consistently lead to a scarcity of food and other resources. The opposite side of this is the forced ceiling imposed by government on wealth creators, since socialism considers a nation's wealth to be a fixed amount instead of capitalism's unleashing of everyone as a wealth creator. By limiting everyone's wealth to a maximum amount, it prevents any individual from developing what some would call "excessive" wealth they can use to either create jobs, increase income levels of their workers, or create foundations which fund companies and nonprofits which benefit the less wealthy.

The other downfall of socialism and social justice programs is the inability of any government or economic system to eliminate poverty. The reality is, there will always be a segment of the population that is less successful than the rest. Even Jesus noted this in Matthew 25:11 when he said, "The poor you will always have with you, but you will not always have me." With some it is a result of mental illness, but there are others who intentionally choose it. Some are even devout Christians who have been taught wealth is evil and poverty is next to Godliness. No matter the reason, all attempts to wipe out poverty are doomed to failure in every culture. That is not to say we should not try to improve the lives of those who have less than ourselves, but it would be wiser to focus on a specific aspect for their lives such as housing or healthcare instead of trying to browbeat them into our personal definitions of success.

The most valid argument presented for Christianity supporting a socialist economy is the indisputable evidence that several of the first churches were communes. There are several references to people selling property (usually just a part) and giving the proceeds to the church who, as Acts 2:44 puts it, "All the believers were together and had everything in common." There are problems with basing an economy on this, which I will point out below.

The first reason is, the early believers were convinced when Jesus said he was returning "soon" it would be in a matter of days or months. This belief led them to focus their energy on reaching out to teach others about Christ instead of earning a living and looking towards a long-term future. While it was important to reach out to others as fast as possible to teach them how to have a personal relationship with God, this quickly led to problems. The church had to appoint a leadership team to take care of widows and orphans, which typically are the first ones neglected as funds begin to run short. As the church expanded and the supply of personal property dwindled, the believers were forced to return to their occupations and the communes broke apart.

The second reason refers to the Jubilee discussed in the Family Second chapter. Every seventy years all property in Israel reverted to the tribe and family who God assigned it to, no matter who they sold it to in the meantime. This kept the land in the hands of the people who God promised it to during their escape from Israel. It also prevented a permanent feudal system from being established, since this happened once every generation. Everyone who sold property to support the early church communes knew they would regain ownership of it if Christ did not return in the short period of time they were expecting.

This leads into another issue which supports the concept of capitalism more than socialism. The basis of capitalism is personal ownership of the economy in all areas—-land, processes, products, and ideas. Socialism believes in the "common" (read government) either owning or controlling everything in the economy. The idea of inheritance is the personal ownership of land and possession, with the understanding it was given by God and should be managed wisely. When people sold property or items to support the early church, it was based on generosity, not forced contributions to fit a five- or ten-year plan by the government.

The last issue I will throw in here is the idea of separation of church and state. This is mentioned in Mark 12:17 which says, "Then Jesus said to them, 'Give back to Caesar what is Caesar's and to God what is God's.' And they were amazed at him." While socialism is discussed as an economic system, it goes far beyond that. It places government above everything else, including expecting the people to have religious devotion to the current and past leaders. It also sets forth the moral code its citizens are expected to follow, usually to the point of pulling children out of the home and indoctrinating them through the education system against any loyalty to either their parents or a religion. The demand for complete loyalty to the government over either religious or family relationships is the opposite of what is taught in Christianity.

The Bible teaches a clear line of loyalty, first to God, then family, and lastly to community, a part of which is government. By prioritizing your relationship with God and following the teachings of Jesus, you will treat your family and community right. You will make it a priority to care for your family and those who are unable to care for themselves, which will largely remove that duty from the government. There are many verses stating you should respect and obey the government, as long as it does not contradict the moral code. This includes paying taxes and, to the consternation of abolitionists everywhere, telling runaway slaves to return to and serve their masters well in areas where slavery was legal. Christianity is all about personal accountability to God first, which forces each believer to maintain a high standard of accountability in the other areas of their lives.

As I have hopefully shown here, Christianity is not an economic model any more than it is a government model. Christianity is about having a personal relationship with God. This relationship is not a stagnant, get-in-and-fall-asleep relationship but one where there is consistent growth and a deepening understanding that surpasses following a list of rules to demonstrating the character of Christ in your everyday interactions with all aspects of society. This relationship does not define an economic model like a textbook or manifesto, but it does help prioritize and focus each political, economic and social organization we are a part of on the correct ideals. How those ideals manifest varies over time and through different models, but it is important to maintain the basic priorities established in our growing relationships with God.

ODDS AND ENDS

In the previous pages we covered the most important theological issues of money management. There are several others that are mentioned only a few times in the Bible, which means they are not fundamental issues but are still good things to pay attention to. This chapter is a quick mention of those issues and why they are relevant to us today. They deal with a wide range of topics, so there will be at least one relevant to your situation somewhere in the list.

Begging:

It is common to see a beggar these days if you live anywhere near a city with a population over twenty thousand. They range from those who drive through and plead for money for gas to those who are local asking for food. For many, begging is the last resort of desperation, while for others it has become a lifestyle to avoid working or to pay for addictions. Many people are uncomfortable around someone begging and will avoid them at all costs by making sure the doors and windows of their cars are locked, crossing the street to avoid them, and refusing to look at them.

How should we as Christians deal with beggars? As we have seen in the chapter on loans, we should be generous and give readily to those in need. Even if we do not have money to give them or are suspicious of their motives, we are directed to treat them with respect and dignity. Paul and Silas demonstrated this in Acts 3:2-10 which tells us, "Now a man who was lame from birth was being carried to the temple gate called Beautiful, where he was put every day to beg from those going into the temple courts. When he saw Peter and John about to enter, he asked them for money. Peter looked straight at him, as did John. Then Peter said, 'Look at us!' So the man gave them his attention, expecting to get something from them. Then Peter said, 'Silver or gold I do not have, but what I do have I give you. In the name of Jesus Christ of Nazareth, walk.' Taking him by the right hand, he helped him up, and instantly the man's feet and ankles became strong. He jumped to his feet and began to walk. Then he went with them into the temple courts, walking and jumping and praising God. When all the people saw him walking and praising God, they recognized him as the same man who used to sit begging at the temple gate called Beautiful, and they were filled with wonder and amazement at what had happened to him."

How should we treat beggars then? As human beings, our equals who have fallen on hard times. In all cases look them in the eyes and smile at them, even if you do not have any money to give them. Taking five minutes to talk to them can change their outlook on life. If you do not have cash but are not in a rush, buy them a meal and eat with them. Find out their story and help them connect with someone who can help them, and above all pray for them before you leave.

Deception:

Deception has become an accepted way of business. This ranges from asking a "reasonable" price for a goat you know is sick to using advertising and social media to drive up demand and the price for a good or service to demanding extreme fees for financial products simply because they are from a specific company. This practice is based on materialism and greed in an attempt to get the most in the shortest amount of time. Here are a few verses warning against following this practice.

> Proverbs 13:11 Dishonest money dwindles away,
>
> but whoever gathers money little by little makes it grow.
>
> Proverbs 20:14 "It's no good, it's no good!" says the buyer—
>
> then goes off and boasts about the purchase.
>
> Proverbs 20:23 The Lord detests differing weights,
>
> and dishonest scales do not please him.

1 Timothy 3:8 In the same way, deacons are to be worthy of respect, sincere, not indulging in much wine, and not pursuing dishonest gain.

The shortcut for avoiding deception is to just be honest. If you sell someone a car you know has an issue let your potential buyer know and adjust the price. Price your products—including pharmaceuticals—based on the cost of development and quality of life they deliver instead of what insurance companies will pay for them. Be happy with a minimum wage if you are working at your first job without experience. Be honest about the product, be honest about your job, be honest about your abilities, and be honest about the effort you put into something.

Discipline:

The key to success in reaching any goal is discipline. Discipline starts with setting the goal, first by making it specific and then in writing it down. That is a great start, but it will not get you there. To reach a specific goal you must learn what it takes to reach it, then break it down into specific baby steps. After you have the steps written down, you must actually do the work and take those steps until you reach the goal. Reaching financial goals requires the same process. Part of the discipline process is being confronted and corrected when we are wrong and learning from it. Here are a few verses which recognize the role discipline plays in reaching financial prosperity.

Psalm 39:11 When you rebuke and discipline anyone for their sin,

you consume their wealth like a moth—

surely everyone is but a breath.

Proverbs 10:4-5 Lazy hands make for poverty,

but diligent hands bring wealth.

He who gathers crops in summer is a prudent son,

but he who sleeps during harvest is a disgraceful son.

Proverbs 13:18 Whoever disregards discipline comes to poverty and shame,

but whoever heeds correction is honored.

Proverbs 15:32-33 Those who disregard discipline despise themselves,

but the one who heeds correction gains understanding.

Wisdom's instruction is to fear the Lord,

and humility comes before honor.

Gambling:

If you grew up in a conservative Christian denomination you were probably taught gambling is evil. This includes things ranging from betting on sports, playing the lottery, and games of chance all the way down to drawings for fundraisers. Some take it so far as to ban the use of dice for playing games because it might somehow lead to gambling in the future. Dave Ramsey calls gambling a "stupid tax", which is an accurate description because the people who can least afford to waste money are the ones who buy the most lottery tickets. While gambling on sports and games of chance almost always results in losing money and is as a rule a bad habit, a Biblical stance against all types of gambling does not exist.

The Bible does not discuss gambling for money directly and focuses on investing instead. However, it does discuss gambling in two different ways. Both ways record common events in society and are mentioned without moral judgement. Here are the accepted ways gambling is mentioned:

The first way the Jews used gambling was to select someone. The selection was done by the religious leaders in both positive and negative ways. In both cases the act of gambling, or casting lots, were trusted by the leaders because they either did not have any way to know the answer or because they believed God would direct the lots better than humans would select the correct person by election. Here are verses that demonstrate this type of gambling.

> Proverbs 16:33 The lot is cast into the lap,
>
> but its every decision is from the Lord.
>
> Proverbs 18:18 Casting the lot settles disputes
>
> and keeps strong opponents apart.
>
> Luke 1:8-9 Once when Zechariah's division was on duty and he was serving as priest before God, he was chosen by lot, according to the custom of the priesthood, to go into the temple of the Lord and burn incense.
>
> Acts 1:26 Then they cast lots, and the lot fell to Matthias; so he was added to the eleven apostles.

The second way gambling was used in the Bible was to divide property. This was done by both religious and political officials. Here are the verses that demonstrate this type of gambling.

> Nahum 3:10 Yet she was taken captive
>
> and went into exile.
>
> Her infants were dashed to pieces
>
> at every street corner.
>
> Lots were cast for her nobles,
>
> and all her great men were put in chains.
>
> Matthew 27:35 When they had crucified him, they divided up his clothes by casting lots.
>
> Mark 15:24 And they crucified him. Dividing up his clothes, they cast lots to see what each would get.

Luke 23:34 Jesus said, "Father, forgive them, for they do not know what they are doing." And they divided up his clothes by casting lots.

John 19:23-24 When the soldiers crucified Jesus, they took his clothes, dividing them into four shares, one for each of them, with the undergarment remaining. This garment was seamless, woven in one piece from top to bottom. "Let's not tear it," they said to one another. "Let's decide by lot who will get it." This happened that the scripture might be fulfilled that said, "They divided my clothes among them and cast lots for my garment." So this is what the soldiers did.

Judging Others:

Christians are supposed to be known by their love, not only for each other but for their neighbors, who Jesus defined as everyone else. Regrettably many Christians are known for their judgmental attitudes more than for their love, concern, and generosity. While the expressed disapproval usually concerns behavior, it can be based on financial issues as well. Inside the church those who fear money can view those who prosper as greedy and using immoral business practices. Those who prosper can view the poor as lazy and wasteful. As we have seen, prosperity or the lack of it is based more on obedience to God and education so we do not have the moral right to judge on either side. Here are some verses that show us the right perspective to take with those whose financial decisions we disagree with.

> 1 Samuel 2:7-8 The Lord sends poverty and wealth;
> he humbles and he exalts.
>
> He raises the poor from the dust
>   and lifts the needy from the ash heap;
> he seats them with princes
>   and has them inherit a throne of honor.
>
> Proverbs 18:21 Do not say, "I'll pay you back for this wrong!"

Wait for the Lord, and he will avenge you.

Proverbs 24:10-12 If you falter in a time of trouble,

how small is your strength!

Rescue those being led away to death;

hold back those staggering toward slaughter.

If you say, "But we knew nothing about this,"

does not he who weighs the heart perceive it?

Does not he who guards your life know it?

Will he not repay everyone according to what they have done?

Matthew 5:25-26 Settle matters quickly with your adversary who is taking you to court. Do it while you are still together on the way, or your adversary may hand you over to the judge, and the judge may hand you over to the officer, and you may be thrown into prison. Truly I tell you, you will not get out until you have paid the last penny.

Sabbath:

The Sabbath is a concept that is generally ignored in industrialized nations. It is notable from a financial perspective in that no business was to be transacted on it. From a wage-earning perspective, the Israelites were even banned from collecting manna on it. While most Christians celebrate their Sabbath on Sunday instead of Saturday, the precept of reserving one day of the week for rest and religious meditation is not only a good idea but is important to maintain our physical and spiritual health.

Where the concept of Sabbath has become muddled is how far it should be taken. With most businesses open every day of the week, is it ok to for Christians to work on Sunday? The most conservative denominations say only if it is necessary for taking care of animals or people, such as farmers and nurses, but not for working in stores. Is it ok for Christians to buy things such as gas, food, or goods on Sunday and essentially force others to work on what should be their day of rest? Ethically no, although if all Christians refused to shop on Sunday they would still have to work because people of other religions (or no religion) would shop then.

Everyone should observe the Sabbath to honor God and become refreshed for the new week. How far you take that observance should be decided after studying the verses about the Sabbath and praying over it before developing your personal conviction. Here are a few relevant verses to chew on to start the process.

> Exodus 16:22-24 On the sixth day, they gathered twice as much—two omers for each person—and the leaders of the community came and reported this to Moses. He said to them, "This is what the Lord commanded: 'Tomorrow is to be a day of sabbath rest, a holy sabbath to the Lord. So bake what you want to bake and boil what you want to boil. Save whatever is left and keep it until morning.'" So they saved it until morning, as Moses commanded, and it did not stink or get maggots in it.

> Exodus 20:7-11 "You shall not misuse the name of the Lord your God, for the Lord will not hold anyone guiltless who misuses his name. "Remember the Sabbath day by keeping it holy. Six days you shall labor and do all your work, but the seventh day is a sabbath to the Lord your God. On it you shall not do any work, neither you, nor your son or daughter, nor your male or female servant, nor your animals, nor any foreigner residing in your towns. For in six days the Lord made the heavens and the earth, the sea, and all that is in them, but he rested on the seventh day. Therefore the Lord blessed the Sabbath day and made it holy.

> Exodus 23:12 For in six days the Lord made the heavens and the earth, the sea, and all that is in them, but he rested on the seventh day. Therefore the Lord blessed the Sab-

bath day and made it holy.

Exodus 35:1-3 Moses assembled the whole Israelite community and said to them, "These are the things the Lord has commanded you to do: For six days, work is to be done, but the seventh day shall be your holy day, a day of sabbath rest to the Lord. Whoever does any work on it is to be put to death. Do not light a fire in any of your dwellings on the Sabbath day."

Leviticus 23:3 There are six days when you may work, but the seventh day is a day of sabbath rest, a day of sacred assembly. You are not to do any work; wherever you live, it is a sabbath to the Lord.

Numbers 15:32-36 While the Israelites were in the wilderness, a man was found gathering wood on the Sabbath day. Those who found him gathering wood brought him to Moses and Aaron and the whole assembly, and they kept him in custody, because it was not clear what should be done to him. Then the Lord said to Moses, "The man must die. The whole assembly must stone him outside the camp." So the assembly took him outside the camp and stoned him to death, as the Lord commanded Moses.

Deuteronomy 5:12-15 "Observe the Sabbath day by keeping it holy, as the Lord your God has commanded you. Six days you shall labor and do all your work, but the seventh day is a sabbath to the Lord your God. On it you shall not do any work, neither you, nor your son or daughter, nor your male or female servant, nor your ox, your donkey or any of your animals, nor any foreigner residing in your towns, so that your male and female servants may rest, as you do. Remember that you were slaves in Egypt and that the Lord your God brought you out of there with a mighty hand and an outstretched arm. Therefore the Lord your God has commanded you to observe the Sabbath day.

Nehemiah 10:31 "When the neighboring peoples bring merchandise or grain to sell on the Sabbath, we will not buy from them on the Sabbath or on any holy day. Every seventh year we will forgo working the land and will cancel all debts.

Matthew 12:1-8 At that time Jesus went through the grainfields on the Sabbath. His disciples were hungry and began to pick some heads of grain and eat them. When the Pharisees saw this, they said to him, "Look! Your disciples are doing what is unlawful on the Sabbath."

Matthew 12:3-8 He answered, "Haven't you read what David did when he and his companions were hungry? He entered the house of God, and he and his companions ate the consecrated bread—which was not lawful for them to do, but only for the priests. Or haven't you read in the Law that the priests on Sabbath duty in the temple desecrate the Sabbath and yet are innocent? I tell you that something greater than the temple is here. If you had known what these words mean, 'I desire mercy, not sacrifice,' you would not have condemned the innocent. For the Son of Man is Lord of the Sabbath."

Matthew 12:9-14 Going on from that place, he went into their synagogue, and a man with a shriveled hand was there. Looking for a reason to bring charges against Jesus, they asked him, "Is it lawful to heal on the Sabbath?"He said to them, "If any of you has a sheep and it falls into a pit on the Sabbath, will you not take hold of it and lift it out? How much more valuable is a person than a sheep! Therefore it is lawful to do good on the Sabbath."Then he said to the man, "Stretch out your hand." So he stretched it out and it was completely restored, just as sound as the other. But the Pharisees went out and plotted how they might kill Jesus.

Colossians 2:16-17 Therefore do not let anyone judge you by what you eat or drink, or with regard to a religious festival, a New Moon celebration or a Sabbath day. These are a shadow of the things that were to come; the reality, however, is found in Christ.

Hebrews 4:8-11 For if Joshua had given them rest, God would not have spoken later about another day. There remains, then, a Sabbath-rest for the people of God; for anyone who enters God's rest also rests from their works, just as God did from his. Let us, therefore, make every effort to enter that rest, so that no one will perish by following their example of disobedience.

Spoils to the Victor:

War is a touchy subject. There are entire denominations who insist Christians should avoid conflict and live as pacifists. On the other hand, there are those who believe they should follow the example of Jesus when he threw out the money changers and merchants from the temple. Even among those who believe war is justified there is a debate over whether the winners should benefit from their victory. The Biblical answer to that is a definite yes. Here are some verses that support it:

Genesis 34:25-29 Three days later, while all of them were still in pain, two of Jacob's sons, Simeon and Levi, Dinah's brothers, took their swords and attacked the unsuspecting city, killing every male. They put Hamor and his son Shechem to the sword and took Dinah from Shechem's house and left. The sons of Jacob came upon the dead bodies and looted the city where their sister had been defiled. They seized their flocks and herds and donkeys and everything else of theirs in the city and out in the fields. They carried off all their wealth and all their women and children, taking as plunder everything in the houses.

Exodus 12:35-36 The Israelites did as Moses instructed and asked the Egyptians for articles of silver and gold and for clothing. The Lord had made the Egyptians favorably disposed toward the people, and they gave them what they asked for; so they plundered the Egyptians.

Joshua 8:2 You shall do to Ai and its king as you did to Jericho and its king, except that you may carry off their plunder and livestock for yourselves. Set an ambush behind the city."

1 Samuel 23:5 So David and his men went to Keilah, fought the Philistines and carried off their livestock. He inflicted heavy losses on the Philistines and saved the people of Keilah.

Isaiah 10:6 I send him against a godless nation,

I dispatch him against a people who anger me,

to seize loot and snatch plunder,

and to trample them down like mud in the streets.

Zechariah 14:14 Judah too will fight at Jerusalem. The wealth of all the surrounding nations will be collected— great quantities of gold and silver and clothing.

Luke 11:21-22 When a strong man, fully armed, guards his own house, his possessions are safe. But when someone stronger attacks and overpowers him, he takes away the armor in which the man trusted and divides up his plunder.

Wisdom:

You can have your relationship with God in the right place and still spend your life in financial crisis if you do not exercise wisdom. Wisdom will drive you to educate yourself about how to manage money through budgeting and carefully choosing your savings and investment options. Wisdom will tell you to consult experts before getting involved in financial agreements, so you avoid unwise business deals. Wisdom will help you prioritize yourself and your family over fads and materialism. In fact, wisdom is more important to have than money and possessions because it will guide you to make the best decisions when you start with nothing. There are many verses saying we should value wisdom, and here are a few of them:

Job 28:12-19 But where can wisdom be found?

Where does understanding dwell?

No mortal comprehends its worth;

it cannot be found in the land of the living.

The deep says, "It is not in me";

the sea says, "It is not with me."

It cannot be bought with the finest gold,

nor can its price be weighed out in silver.

It cannot be bought with the gold of Ophir,

with precious onyx or lapis lazuli.

Neither gold nor crystal can compare with it,

nor can it be had for jewels of gold.

Coral and jasper are not worthy of mention;

the price of wisdom is beyond rubies.

The topaz of Cush cannot compare with it;

it cannot be bought with pure gold.

Proverbs 2:1-5 My son, if you accept my words

and store up my commands within you,

turning your ear to wisdom

and applying your heart to understanding—

indeed, if you call out for insight

and cry aloud for understanding,

and if you look for it as for silver

and search for it as for hidden treasure,

then you will understand the fear of the Lord

and find the knowledge of God.

Proverbs 10:14 The wise store up knowledge,

but the mouth of a fool invites ruin.

Proverbs 12:15 The way of fools seems right to them,

but the wise listen to advice.

Proverbs 16:16 How much better to get wisdom than gold,

to get insight rather than silver!

Proverbs 24:3-4 By wisdom a house is built,

and through understanding it is established;

through knowledge its rooms are filled

with rare and beautiful treasures.

Ecclesiastes 7:11-12 Wisdom, like an inheritance, is a good thing

and benefits those who see the sun.

Wisdom is a shelter

as money is a shelter,

but the advantage of knowledge is this:

Wisdom preserves those who have it.

Colossians 2:2-3 My goal is that they may be encouraged in heart and united in love, so that they may have the full riches of complete understanding, in order that they may know the mystery of God, namely, Christ, in whom are hidden all the treasures of wisdom and knowledge.

WHY IS IT SO HARD?

Why is managing finances effectively so hard? The obvious answer is the complexity of the options available. There are several types of investments that sound very attractive during the sales pitch but should not even be considered unless you are highly educated and experienced in financial issues. The language used by financial professionals is confusing to the point the same tools available are called different names by different companies. With the culture of hidden costs and fees, it is almost impossible to accurately compare similar products to determine which are the most effective ones to choose. On top of that, each person's personality determines what types of tools they are open to using, so each person needs to find someone who will take the time to understand what they are comfortable with, analyze what they need now and in retirement, and create a realistic plan to reach those goals.

I spent a lot of time trying to come up with a good comparison for how most people manage their finances to something most people would understand. Then, as I got older, I developed Type 2 Diabetes—partially due to genetics. It took me a few years to understand how fitting this disease is to how many people manage their money, but the similarities are incredible. Here is what I mean:

Type 2 Diabetes is a condition where your body either runs out of insulin, or your body becomes so accustomed to having so much insulin dumped into your system because of sugar and carbohydrate overdosing that your cells become resistant to it. The condition used to only show up later in life, but because of high concentrations of sugars, carbohydrates, and artificial chemicals in pre-packaged and restaurant foods, it is now becoming common in teenagers. The disease is "silent" until the person maxes out their production or tolerance for insulin, but every meal they eat contributes to their deterioration. Every time they drink a soda, eat a high-fat meal, eat a larger portion than they need (like that extra trip to the buffet) or do not eat a balanced diet, they bring themselves one step closer to crossing the line. There is plenty of dietary education out there about the dangers of not eating right or the right portions, but most people just ignore it. One of the medications I currently take costs $500—after insurance covers their part. If we could move everyone forward thirty years and show them the consequences of their current eating patterns it would make a dramatic difference, but that is impossible. We might make dramatic changes in our eating habits if we understood each soda we drink is going to cost us $20.00 for medication in the future, and each extra trip through the buffet line is going to cost us $50.00 in the future.

Not having a financial plan, or not following the plan we have, affects our financial future the same way poor eating habits affect our medical future. Every time we splurge on a specialty coffee, buy clothes we do not need, or go out to eat is the equivalent of a sugar bomb in our retirement plans—relatively unnoticeable when we do it but building towards a disaster in the future. Eventually buying outside the lines starts blowing up our credit cards, or we borrow money against our homes to cover the extra expenses. Suddenly we are ten years from retiring, and the financial expert tells us retirement at the minimum age is not possible. All those financial sugar bombs we dropped through the years have destroyed the financial insulin (interest and returns) that should have been building up in financial tools to achieve our goals. To make up for the lost returns we should have had, the $1 of investment we should have made when we were twenty now must be replaced with at least $50 of current income. As with diabetes, there is plenty of financial education out there we could have used over the years, but we choose to focus on getting Stuff and trying to impress our friends and neighbors instead.

From a religious perspective, finances start out being hard. When we first give our lives to Christ, we continue juggling the financial tools we have always used and throw a religious veneer over them, starting with tithing. Instead of making managing finances easier, it makes it more complex by seemingly trying to do the same with ten percent less. The pressures of squeezing in your current expenditures increases not only with tithing but also with being generous to those around you. The stress of keeping all the plates spinning gets worse as unexpected expenses shrink your available assets.

The struggle of managing finances starts to get easier the same way your life improves in any other area. The only way to permanently improve your finances is to allow Christ to take control of them. Once Christ is in the driver's seat, your financial life will simplify in many ways such as:

1. Your career choice will be based on the direction God leads you or, if there is not a specific leading, the talents and abilities he has given you.

2. Tithing becomes easy since you understand and appreciate that God has given you everything.

3. Educated generosity towards others is a natural outgrowth of living a Christian life.

4. You will understand money is a neutral tool and takes on the moral connotations of what you choose to use it for.

5. You understand you have a moral obligation to earn a living and use your earnings to support your immediate family.

6. It will be easier to humble yourself to the point you acknowledge your understanding of finances is inadequate, so you will take the time and effort to educate yourself about them and consult professionals before making significant purchases or investments.

7. You understand honesty is key to success and will not overcharge others, charge them excess interest, or misrepresent your contributions in financial deals.

8. Being content with what you have removes the lust of materialism and allows you the luxury of time to save for future purchases of things you need instead of chasing fads.

9. Understanding the value of things allows us to appreciate what we have and carefully choose to purchase only those things that add value to your life or those around you in the context of serving God.

10. If you must get a loan for something, you will carefully evaluate the value of what you are buying and find the best loan terms before committing to it.

11. You understand retirement is a Biblical concept and not only educate yourself about your savings and investment choices but also obtain the advice of experienced professionals to reach your goals.

12. You understand that it is a Biblical command to accumulate more than what you will need for retirement so you can provide a financial legacy for your children.

13. You will value the contributions of others who assist you in meeting your financial goals regardless of their sex or race. You will value those who support your own endeavors, especially your spouse.

14. You will appreciate the value of all humans no matter what their financial circumstances are and treat them respectfully.

15. Even if you accumulate significant wealth, you will recognize that your value to God has nothing to do with the amount of assets you have but by how you fulfil God's leadings in your life and how you treat other people.

16. Acknowledge God as the source of your life, talents, abilities, and finances by tithing ten percent of your gross income to the local religious organization you are a consistent and active part of.

17. Demonstrate concern for your neighbors both near and far by giving of your time and finances to improve their physical and mental conditions.

18. Be a good steward of your financial resources by living frugally in the present and planning and funding your future needs on the remaining eighty five percent or less of your net income. Constantly educate yourself to utilize the most efficient and least costly tools so you can direct more of your resources towards others.

19. Be content with what you have right now. Although it is healthy to dream and plan for the future, dissatisfaction with what you have without action to improve yourself leads to cheating, deception, bribery, and other attempts to shortcut your path to prosperity.

20. Provide for your family first, even if it means sacrificing current de-

sires. Protecting your family with life and health insurance and healthy foods is more important than having a boat to take everyone out to the lake on every weekend.

21. The first step to Biblical prosperity is to turn your entire life and all your resources over to God. This is an ongoing process, initially acknowledged through tithing.

22. As you become more prosperous, increase your generosity faster than your lifestyle spending. Prosperity can be fleeting and is typically one of the first casualties of ego overcoming valuing your true source.

The number of financial tools available are staggering and only increases with time. While some instruments available today will be retired as fee and performance disclosures become stricter, more will take their place. It is almost impossible to keep up with all of the changes unless that is your job, and even then many chose to focus on specific products and ignore the rest. The one thing you can be sure of is if you are grounded in the fundamental spiritual aspect of giving God control over your finances the Holy Spirit will actively guide your choices over time to lead you to prosperity in all areas of your life.

APPENDIX

Tools For Success

Here is a brief overview of several financial tools available to help reach your financial goals. My first, and most important, message is although there are many tools you should utilize those best suited to your personality and knowledge level. Despite the claims of some financial gurus, one set of financial tools does not fit all. The tools you should use are defined by your age, current resources, and personal goals.

While it is convenient to start out using certain tools as a teenager, it is not only naïve but also dangerous to your ongoing financial wellbeing to only use those tools your entire life. The first reason it is dangerous I mentioned above, in that needs and tolerance for risk change over time. The second reason is, like depending on hand-forged wrenches when air sockets are available, the financial industry continually reinvents itself to stay competitive and relevant. While many of these reinventions are simple re-brandings, there are some significant steps forward that should be taken advantage of when they occur. That is why you should never accept one financial philosophy teaching everyone should do x and y and stick to it for the rest your life. I recommend you make it a point to update your financial knowledge by not only reading this book (thank you) but by taking Financial Peace University by Dave Ramsey, Crown Financial, and any other Christian and secular financial resource you can find. In the meantime, coffee shops will thank you because most of the programs are painfully similar with a couple outlying thoughts, which I recommend you evaluate with an experienced financial professional.

Here is a list of some financial tools available with a brief summary of how they work. Each one is useful in some circumstances and worthless in others, so you should educate yourself and consult someone experienced with them before utilizing any of them.

Savings account: offered by banks and some insurance companies. Although they are safe, they have the lowest rates of return and are taxed yearly unless they are set up under an Individual Retirement Account (IRA).

Certificate of Deposit: offered by banks. They have higher rates of return than savings accounts in return for locking in the deposit for an extended period. Interest earned is taxable if they are not in an IRA. There are penalties for early withdrawals.

Bonds: debt instruments (basically shares in a loan) for companies and governments. The yield is inversely proportional to interest rates, i.e. when interest rates go up the yield decreases. The greatest risk is if the holder pays off the loan early, your returns immediately end.

- Local and state government bonds: may be exempt from state income taxes, but it depends on how it is issued.

- Federal and corporate bonds: fully taxed.

Stocks: partial ownership in a company. Gains and losses are taxable every year if they are held outside of an IRA. Stocks must be traded through brokerage firms who charge either a commission or yearly fee in addition to yearly management fees.

Classes of stocks:

- Preferred: typically has a fixed dividend. If the company is liquidated, they have first priority on the proceeds.

- Common: each stock has one voting right in the company. Dividends are variable based on the board's vote. If the company is liquidated, they get an equal share of what is left after the preferred shareholders are paid.

Types of stocks:

- Income: bought and held for the dividends they pay. They typically have little focus on growth.

- Growth: bought with the expectation of their value increasing significantly. They typically have little expectation of dividends.

- Penny: small companies that are purchased on a long shot of them growing significantly or being bought out.

Mutual funds: funds of mixtures of stocks and/or bonds put together by investment advisors hired by brokerages to meet specific objectives. Mutual funds charge all the stock fees with an additional fee for the money managers. Taxes are paid yearly unless they are under an IRA or other qualified retirement plan.

Types of mutual funds:

- Money market: a mix of short-term income instruments such as loans for companies to buy goods, government bonds and CDs. Yields are slightly higher than CDs and are taxable annually unless they are in an IRA.

- Fixed income: a mix of government and/or corporate bonds focused on steady returns.

- Investment: a mix of stocks and/or bonds. Each investment mutual fund is set up to achieve a specific goal, which is stated in the fund's prospectus. Generally focused on growth which is driven by the market and will include losses.

- Balanced: a mix of stocks or bonds designed to have moderate growth with reduced losses.

- Foreign: a mix of stocks from other countries. They have a higher risk than domestic funds. Although the risk is higher, they generally move opposite domestic funds so they can help balance risk.

- Specialty: a mix of funds designed to achieve a specific purpose. Common ones are designed around either conscience (avoid alcohol, tobacco, and drug companies) or social action (green technologies).

- Index: purchased on one of the exchanges (Dow Jones, S&P 500, etc.). Each share has an equal portion of every stock sold on the exchange or a representative sample of them with the expectation the overall fund will have positive results, i.e. the number of stocks gaining in value will outnumber the number of stocks losing value.

Retirement Plans:

There are many retirement plans available. Each has its own legal definitions and restrictions. While balances generally go up every year, most of it is due to contributions instead of earnings. To find out what you earned in a year, subtract the previous year's balance from the end-of-year total, then subtract what you have contributed from that. Divide the difference by the previous year's balance to find out what percentage you have earned after fees. Funds are unavailable until age 65 without a 10% penalty and income tax payment.

Business:

- Traditional 401k: plans created for larger private businesses. Participants chose from a limited number of mutual funds. Costs and fees are difficult to determine. Contributions are frequently matched up to a certain percentage, which is free money you should take advantage of. Plans are based on annuities. Contributions are not taxed, but all withdrawals are taxed as ordinary income.

- ROTH 401k: similar to a traditional plan except taxes are paid on all contributions, and withdrawals are tax free.

- Small business: stock investment plans created for businesses with less than one hundred employees. These include KEOGH, SIMPLE, and SEP plans. The size of the business and how contributions are made determines what the best plan is for each business. Contributions are not taxed, but all withdrawals are taxed as ordinary income.

- Indexed: insurance-based plan which is based on annuities. Money is not in the market so there is no loss of principal from changes in the market. Contributions are taxed as ordinary income, but withdrawals are only taxed on the growth.

Government and Non-profit:

- Traditional 403b: comparable to a Traditional 401k.

- ROTH 403b: comparable to a ROTH 401k.

- Indexed: comparable to a business Indexed plan.

Personal:

- Traditional IRA: most plans are invested in mutual funds, although other things can be incorporated into it. Plans have yearly fees on top of the investment fees of the funds utilized. Contributions are not taxed, but all investments risk loss in the market and are subject to future tax law changes. Plan withdrawals are determined by the account holder and are usually exhausted within 6 years.

- ROTH IRA: similar to Traditional IRAs except all contributions are taxed and all withdrawals are tax free.

- Tax-Free Retirement: insurance-based retirement program similar to an Indexed plan.

Life insurance:

All life insurance is based on a basic term (one year) policy which renews every year. Life insurance is cheap when you are young and increases dramatically as you get older until the cost for one year of insurance is extremely high after age 65. The more medical conditions you develop as you age increases your risk of death, which also increases your cost. When you purchase life insurance, the company calculates your risk of death over the number of years the policy lasts and your current health and charges you based on that risk. Your premium for most policies is calculated based on your increasing risk and divided out so it stays the same. Insurance that is designed to last your entire life includes some type of savings or investment vehicle to build cash value.

It is necessary to mention life insurance policies on children. Some people are adamantly opposed to the idea, claiming you will benefit from the death of your child. While there may be some truth to this, it misses a few things. First, it covers funeral expenses if something does happen to your child—which avoids community fundraisers and Go Fund Me accounts. Second, it is increasingly common for children to develop devastating health conditions such as Type I diabetes, which permanently disqualifies them from purchasing life insurance. Third, the cash value in life insurance is not counted as an asset when filing for college education loans and can be borrowed from to cover those expenses without paying taxes on it. Lastly, if you take out the right kind of policy on a young child, the cash value can continue growing, and the child takes over ownership of it until it supplements their retirement income. For those four reasons it is important to insure children as young as possible and utilize it as a tool to ease their financial journey if it becomes necessary.

Types of life insurance:

- Term: straight life insurance. Usually sold in increments of 5, 10, 15, or 20 years. This is least expensive life insurance when you are young but will cost you hundreds of dollars a year after the age of seventy because of your high risk of death.

- Whole life: insurance with a savings option the company invests at their discretion in low-risk instruments such as bonds and CDs.

- Universal life: insurance with the cash value growing in a money market account.

- Variable life: insurance with the cash value invested in mutual funds the customer selects through the company. Since the cash is invested in stocks you not only must pay the stock investment fees but you have market risk.

- Indexed life: insurance with the cash value performance linked to a market index, such as the S&P 500. The cash value is not directly invested in the market so you do not have market losses but benefit from market gains.

Insurance terms:

- Guaranteed renewability: most term life insurance has guaranteed renewability, which means the company has to offer to renew your policy when it expires. What most people do not understand is the premium adjusts to reflect your current risk, which is frequently twice as much for the new term even if you do not have to redo your health screen.

- Credit insurance: a term life policy for the length of a loan, especially a mortgage. The loan company takes out the insurance on the borrower to recover the cost of the loan if they should die before it is paid off.

- Rider: a supplemental policy for additional cost. Common ones are to cover children until age 20 and return of premium which guarantees your cash value will equal (not necessarily exceed) what you have paid into the policy.

- Living benefits: options for utilizing part of your life insurance face vale while you are still alive. This varies significantly among companies, and many cancel the policy if you utilize this option, so it is important to understand what the company means by living benefits before purchasing the policy. Living benefits are triggered by specific medical conditions, and each company sets their own qualifications for them and how much they will pay out for those conditions. Living benefit payments are made to the policyholder. The types of Living Benefits are listed below:

  - Loan option: some companies call your ability to borrow against your cash value a living benefit.

  - Chronic illness: if you develop a chronic illness such as MS or ALS you can access part of your face amount for a set number of months to help cover medical costs, living expenses, or experimental treatments.

  - Critical illness: if you experience a critical illness such as a heart attack you can access part of your face amount to help cover medical costs and living expenses while you are off work.

  - Terminal illness: if you develop an illness and you are not expected to live more than one or two years, you can access part of your face amount to cover medical costs, living expenses, or a bucket list vacation with your family.

Long term care insurance:

Insurance to cover treatment for specific health issues. Payments are made directly to the health provider. Since most policies are purchased later in life when the risk of health issues is high, they are expensive. Many people fail to qualify for this type of insurance because of health issues they already have when they apply for a policy.

Real Estate Investment Trusts (REIT):

Companies who own several commercial buildings may bundle their holdings and sell partial ownership of the buildings to investors. These used to be relatively safe investments but with cultural shifts away from malls and shopping centers, it is important to investigate these carefully before becoming involved.

Real estate:

There are many sources out there urging people to invest in real estate. Some even say you can do it without any money down. The truth is real estate runs in cycles, is money intensive, and takes time and expertise to make money in. My personal experience reflects that of many others in that real estate should be avoided unless you have enough money put away to pay for the property for months or even years and have the time and expertise to do most of the work on it yourself.

- Flipping houses: takes time and money to purchase and remodel. Sometimes problems show up that are costly to fix and eat into the profit margin. No matter how much money you put into a place it is only worth what someone else is willing to pay for it.

- Rentals: most rentals require repairs. Many renters are lax in taking care of a property so maintenance and repair costs can be significant. Problem renters are difficult to evict, even when their leases have expired. It is key to have a competent attorney draw up the rental contract to close loopholes and abide by local laws.

Emergency Fund:

An emergency fund is enough cash to cover at least six months of expenses in the event you become ill or lose your source of income. It is vital to have a fully funded emergency fund as part of your financial toolbox.

Budget:

A budget is a spreadsheet that tracks money coming into and going out of home or business. While it is important to keep track of your finances, it will just keep you broke unless it includes savings for maintaining your home and transportation and providing for retirement in the future.

Financial Plan:

A financial plan incorporates your current and future needs into how your money is used. Vehicles need oil changes and new tires periodically and occasional larger maintenance which needs to be planned for. Vacations, Christmas, and birthdays occur every year and need to be included. Houses always need some sort of attention along with new water heaters, furnaces, and air conditioners every five to ten years and new roofs every twenty years or so that need to be planned for. People get sick, so not only do you need to be able to cover medical expenses but also daily expenses while you are unable to work. A true financial plan covers all current and future expenses which means making daily sacrifices until adequate savings and investments have been made.

Personal suggestions:

I have been involved in the financial services industry for about 20 years. I have for various lengths of time been a life insurance agent, supervising broker for mutual funds in a small office, and a mortgage loan agent. During this time I have seen the cost of life insurance drop dramatically, several new highs set in the market along with it dropping by around 50% in one year—twice, and a majority of small mortgage companies and investment brokers eliminated by increased fees because of one federal law being passed. Based on my experiences here are my suggestions to accumulate wealth in the safest and most efficient manner—after you have settled your spiritual war, of course.

1. Create a financial plan. This is the bedrock of your financial house and must prioritize tithing and giving. It should be reviewed annually and

modified to reflect any major life changes.

2. Create a budget. This is the basement of your financial house and tracks what your money is used for, including all the items and priorities of your financial plan. Budgets are not set in stone but should only be modified if absolutely necessary.

3. Protect your family and your income. The first floor of your financial house is best built with a Living Benefits term life insurance policy, which is the least expensive way to not only create an artificial estate if something happens but help cover catastrophic medical costs for certain conditions to prevent bankruptcies.

4. Build a supplemental retirement income source that can be tapped for medical expenses if the Living Benefits term policy is exhausted. This is the second floor of your financial house and is accomplished with a Living Benefits Indexed life insurance policy.

5. Once you have secured adequate retirement funds, invest directly in the market. The roof of your financial house is owning stocks and bonds, which allows you to accumulate additional wealth and stimulate the economy at the same time. This is partially built through investing in your company's retirement plan and their matching contributions.

Figure 5

HOUSE OF FINANCIAL SUCCESS

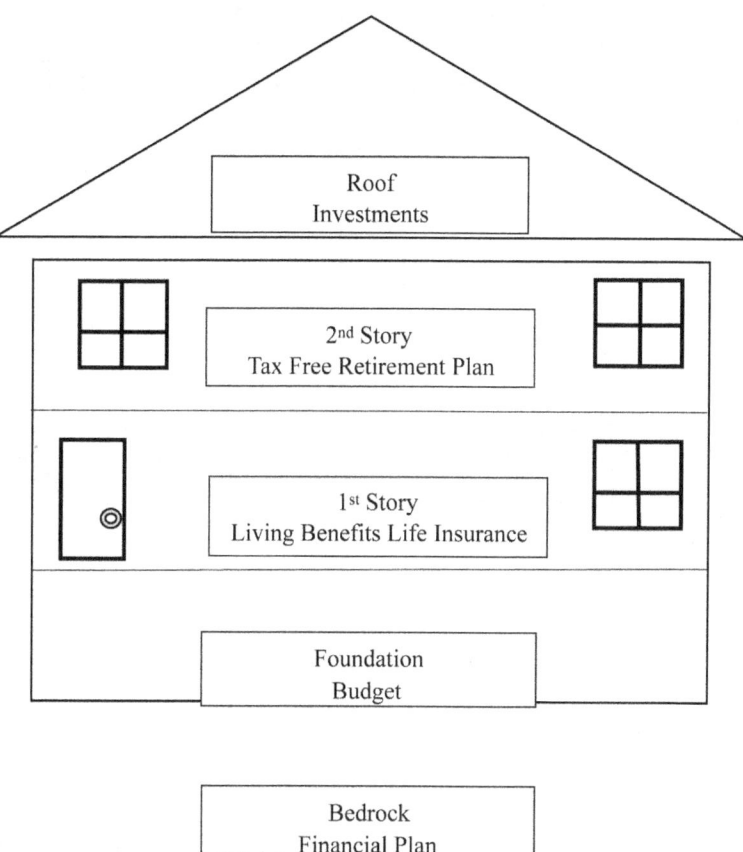

I call this bibliography exhausting rather than exhaustive. It took a couple hundred hours to put together, but I cannot guarantee it contains all the relevant Bible verses or that the verses are all under the most appropriate categories. I only hope it aids you as you continue your search for clarity in your own pursuit of financial understanding.

Begging
1 Samuel 2:36; Acts 3:2-10

Blessing
Deuteronomy 11:26-28; 1 Kings 3:10-15; Job 36:5-12; Job 36:16-21; Job 42:10-15; Psalms 1:1-3; Psalms 21:3-7; Psalms 24:3-6; Psalms 37:28-29; Psalms 92:12-15; Psalms 112:1-5; Psalms 115:12-13; Psalms 128; Psalms 144:13-15; Proverbs 2:21-22; Proverbs 3; Proverbs 10:4-5; Proverbs 10:22; Proverbs 24:23-25; Isaiah 61:7; Malachi 3:8-12

Borrow
Exodus 22:14; Exodus 22:15; Deuteronomy 15:6; Deuteronomy 28:12; 2 Kings 6:5; Nehemiah 5:4; Psalms37:21; Proverbs 22:7; Isaiah 24:2; Jeremiah 15:10; Matthew 5:42

Bribe
Numbers 22:16-18; Numbers 24:10-13; Deuteronomy 10:7; Deuteronomy 27:25; Judges 16:4-5, 18; 1 Samuel 8:1-3; 1 Samuel 12:3-5; Esther 3:9, 11; Esther 4:7; Esther 7:3-4; Psalms 15:5; Psalms 17:4; Psalms 17:4; Psalms 26:9-11; Proverbs 17:8; Proverbs 17:23; Proverbs 21:17; Proverbs 29:4; Ecclesiastes 7:7; Isaiah 1:23; Isaiah 33:15-16; Ezekiel 22:12; Amos 5:12; Micah 3:11; Micah 7:3; Matthew 27:3-10; Matthew 28:12-15; Acts 8:18-24; Acts 24:26

Cheating
Genesis 31:1-16; Genesis 31:43; Deuteronomy 25:13-17; Proverbs 11:1; Proverbs 20:10; Hosea 12:7-8; Amos 8:4-6; Matthew 10:18-22; 1 Corinthians 5:11; 1 Corinthians 6:7-8

Compassion
Job 22:7-11; Job 29:11-17; Job 31:16-23; Psalms 103:8-12; Proverbs 21:13

Contentment
Philippians 4:12-13

Cost
2 Kings 6:24-25; 2 Kings 7:1-2; 2 Kings 7:8, 16; Proverbs 23:6-8; 1 Corinthians 9:7; 1 Corinthians 9:17-18; Revelation 21:6-7

Covet
Deuteronomy 5:21; Deuteronomy 7:25; Joshua 7:20-25; Proverbs 12:12; Acts 20:32-35; Romans 7:7-12; Romans 13:8-10; James 4:2-3

Craft
2 Chronicles 2:7; 2 Chronicles 2:13-14; Nehemiah 3:8; Nehemiah 3:31-32; Ezekiel 27:9; Zechariah 6:10-12

Curse
Deuteronomy 28:15-68; Judges 2:14; Judges 3:7-8; Judges 4:1-2; Judges 6:1-6; 2 Chronicles 24:20; Nehemiah 9:36-37; Job 8:2-7; Job 15:27-29; Job 20:4-29; Job 27:16-19; Job 31:2-3; Job 31:5-8; Job 31:16-23; Job 36:5-12; Psalms 1:4-6; Psalms 11:5-6; Psalms 37:14-17; Psalms 37:28-29; Psalms 92:6-7; Psalms 105:16-19; Psalms 105:25-38; Psalms 109:20; Proverbs 1:28-33; Proverbs 2:21-22; Proverbs 3; Proverbs 10:2; Proverbs 24:23-25; Jeremiah 16:18; Jeremiah 17:5-8; Haggai 2:16; Malachi 2:1-2

Debt
1 Samuel 22:2; Luke 16:1-15; Romans 13:8-10; Colossians 2:13-15; Philippians 1:18-19

Deception
Genesis 42:25-28; Genesis 42:35; Genesis 44:1-13; Proverbs 1:13-16; Proverbs 13:11; Proverbs 16:11; Proverbs 20:14; Proverbs 20:17; Proverbs 20:23; Proverbs 21:6; Jeremiah 17:11; Micah 2:2; Micah 6:10-15; Malachi 3:5; Acts 5:1-11; 1 Timothy 3:8; 1 Timothy 6:2-10; Titus 1:7; Titus 1:10; 1 Peter 5:1-4

Dedicated Item Value
Leviticus 27:1-29; Numbers 3:11-13; Numbers 3:44-51; 1 Kings 15:15; Ecclesiastes 12:6-7

Discipline
Psalms 39:11; Proverbs 10:4-5; Proverbs 13:18; Proverbs 15:32-33

Dowry
Genesis 25:52-53; 1 Samuel 18:23-27

Earnings
Proverbs 10:15-16; Proverbs 11:18; Proverbs 11:30-31; Proverbs 12:11; Proverbs 12:14; Proverbs 12:27; Proverbs 14:23; Proverbs 15:6; Proverbs 22:4; Proverbs 27:23-27; Proverbs 28:19; Proverbs 31:18; Proverbs 31:24; Ecclesiastes 11:1-2; Isaiah 5:8-10; Isaiah 23:2-3; Isaiah 23:17-18; Jeremiah 22:13; Micah 1:7; Micah 3:11; Habakkuk 2:13; Haggai 1:5-6; Zechariah 8:10; Zechariah 11:12-13; Malachi 3:5; Matthew 20:1-16; Matthew 21:33-41; Matthew 14:3-9; Luke 3:14; John 4:34-38; Acts 16:16-21; Acts 19:23-27; Acts 20:32-35; Romans 4:4-5; 2 Thessalonians 3:7-15; 1 Timothy 5:18; 2 Timothy 2:6; James 5:1-6; 2 Peter 2:13-16

Envy
Psalms 73:3-11; Proverbs 23:17-18

Extortion
Jeremiah 22:15-17; Ezekiel 18:18; Ezekiel 22:12; Ezekiel 22:29; Habakkuk 2:6-9; Luke 3:14

Futile
Job 6:13; Psalms 39:6; Proverbs 11:28; Proverbs 23:4-5; Ecclesiastes 3:3-4

Gambling
Proverbs 16:33; Proverbs 18:18; Nahum 3:10; Matthew 27:35; Mark 15:24; Luke 1:8-9; Luke 23:34; John 19:23-24; Acts 1:26

Generosity
Psalms 37:25-26; Proverbs 11:24-26; Proverbs 12:10; Proverbs 14:18; Proverbs 14:31; Proverbs 21:25-26; Proverbs 22:9; Proverbs 25:21-22; Proverbs 27:10; Proverbs 28:27; Proverbs 31:20; Matthew 25:34-46; Luke 6:30; Luke 6:38; Luke 11:41; Acts 4:33-37; Acts 5:1-11; Acts 10:2; Romans 15:26-28; 2 Corinthians 8:1-5; 2 Corinthians 9:6-15; 1 John 3:17-18

Gift
Genesis 25:22; Genesis 25:52-53; Genesis 43:1-26; Genesis 45:22-23; Genesis 47:11-12; 1 Samuel 10:26-27; 1 Samuel 25:20-27; 2 Samuel 11:8; 1 Kings 10:1-12; 1 Kings 10:13; 1 Kings 10:24-25; 1 Kings 13:7-

10; 1 Kings 14:1-3; 2 Kings 5:4-27; 2 Kings 8:7-8; 2 Kings 16:7-9; 1 Chronicles 29:1-9; 2 Chronicles 5:1; 2 Chronicles 9:1; 2 Chronicles 9:9-12; 2 Chronicles 15:18; 2 Chronicles 17:3-6; 2 Chronicles 21:2; Ezra 1:4, 6; Ezra 1:7-11; Ezra 2:68-69; Ezra 5:13-15; Ezra 6:5; Esther 9:20-22; Psalms 45:10-15; Psalms 68:18; Psalms 68:28-31; Psalms 72:10-11; Psalms 72:15; Psalms 76:7-12; Proverbs 18:16; Proverbs 19:6; Proverbs 21:14; Proverbs 22:16; Isaiah 18:7; Isaiah 39:1-2; Isaiah 60:5-17; Ezekiel 16:32-34; Ezekiel 20:26; Ezekiel 20:31; Ezekiel 20:39-40; Ezekiel 45:13-17; Ezekiel 46:16-18; Daniel 2:6; Daniel 2:48; Daniel 5:17; Micah 1:7; Micah 1:14; Micah 3:5; Micah 7:3; Matthew 2:11; Matthew 5:23-24; Matthew 6:1-4; Matthew 7:7-12; Matthew 8:4; Matthew 23:16-22; Luke 11:13; Luke 21:5; John 4:10; Acts 10:4; Acts 11:29-30; Romans 4:4-5; Romans 5:15-17; 2 Corinthians 8:12-15; 2 Corinthians 8:19-21; 2 Corinthians 9:1-5; 2 Corinthians 9:6-15; 2 Corinthians 11:7-9; Ephesians 2:8-10; Ephesians 3:7; Ephesians 4:8; Philippians 4:15-19; 1 Timothy 4:14; Hebrews 5:1-4; Hebrews 6:4-6; Hebrews 8:3-4; Hebrews 9:9-10; 1 Peter 5:10; Revelation 11:10; Revelation 22:17

Giving
Deuteronomy 15:7-11; 1 Chronicles 29:14-18; Psalms 112:9; Proverbs 25:14; Proverbs 25:21-22; Proverbs 28:22; Romans 12:6-8; 2 Corinthians 9:1-5; 2 Corinthians 9:6-15; Philippians 4:15-19

God Judges
1 Samuel 2:7-8; Psalms 28:4-5; Psalms 76:7-12; Psalms 82:2-4; Psalms 82:8; Proverbs 18:21; Proverbs 22:22-23; Proverbs 24:10-12; Proverbs 30:10

Greed
Job 24:1-3; Job 24:13-21; Psalms 119:36; Psalms 127:1-2; Proverbs 15:27; Proverbs 28:20; Proverbs 28:25; Ecclesiastes 4:5-6; Ecclesiastes 5:8-20; Jeremiah 6:13; Ezekiel 33:31; Micah 2:2; Micah 6:10-15; Luke 12:13-15; Acts 1:28-32; 1 Corinthians 5:11; Ephesians 5:3-7; Colossians 3:5; 1 Timothy 3:4-5; 1 Timothy 6:2-10; 2 Timothy 3:1-5; Hebrews 13:5; 2 Peter 2:13-16

Harvest
Isaiah 17:5-6; Isaiah 17:10-11; Isaiah 18:4-5; Jeremiah 2:3; Jeremiah 2:5-7; Jeremiah 6:9; Jeremiah 8:13; Jeremiah 12:13; Ezekiel 34:27-28;

Amos 7:1-2; Micah 4:12; Micah 7:1; Habakkuk 3:17; Haggai 1:5-6; Haggai 1:11; Zechariah 8:12; Matthew 21:33-41; Mark 4:8; Mark 4:20; Mark 4:29; Mark 12:1-9; Luke 8:8; Luke 8:15; Luke 10:2-4; Luke 12:16-21; Luke 19:9-16; John 4:34-38; 1 Corinthians 9:9-13; 2 Corinthians 9:6-15; Galatians 6:9; 2 Timothy 2:6; Hebrews 6:7-8; James 5:7; Revelations 14:14-20; Revelations 22:1-2

Honesty

Exodus 20:15; Leviticus 25:14-17; Proverbs 11:1; Proverbs 12:5; Proverbs 16:11; Proverbs 28:16; Proverbs 28:18; Jeremiah 5:1-2; Ezekiel 45:10-12; Matthew 23:16-22

Idolatry

Exodus 20:22-23; Judges 8:23-27; Judges 17:1-4; Judges 17:10; Judges 14:14-21; Psalms 115:3-8; Psalms 135:15-18; Isaiah 2:20; Isaiah 30:22; Isaiah 31:6-7; Isaiah 40:19-20; Isaiah 44:9-20; Jeremiah 2:5-7; Jeremiah 2:11; Jeremiah 10:3-5; Jeremiah 10:8-9; Jeremiah 10:14-15; Jeremiah 51:17-18; Ezekiel 16:17; Daniel 3:1-18; Daniel 5:23; Hosea 8:6; Hosea 13:2; Habakkuk 2:18-19; Acts 17:29; Acts 19:23-27; Revelation 9:20

Impartial

Job 34:16-20; Proverbs 24:28-29; Proverbs 25:11-12; Proverbs 28:21; Proverbs 29:4; Proverbs 29:13-14; Proverbs 31:8-9; Isaiah 46:6-7; Isaiah 48:5

Inheritance

Genesis 15:1-3; Genesis 48:3-4; Exodus 6:6-8; Exodus 15:17; Leviticus 25:23-24; Numbers 18:20; Numbers 26:52-56; Numbers 27:8-11; Numbers 32:2-5; Numbers 32:18-22; Numbers 32:28-33; Numbers 35:1-8; Numbers 36:1-12; Deuteronomy 9:4-6; Deuteronomy 10:9; Deuteronomy 12:10; Deuteronomy 19:8-9; Deuteronomy 21:15-17; Deuteronomy 31:7-8; Joshua 11:23; Joshua 13:6-8; Joshua 13:14, 32-33; Joshua 14:1-5; Joshua 14:9, 13; Joshua 15:20; Joshua 16:4-9; Joshua 17:4-6; Joshua 17:14; Joshua 18:1-7; Joshua 18:20; Joshua 19:1, 9; Joshua 19:10, 16; Joshua 19:23; Joshua 19:31; Joshua 19:39; Joshua 19:48; Joshua 19:49-50; Joshua 23:4-5; Joshua 24:28-29; Joshua 24:32; Judges 2:6-8; Judges 11:1-2; Judges 18:1; Judges 21:23-24; 1 Samuel 10:1; 1 Samuel 26:17-19; 2 Samuel 14:16-17; 2 Samuel 20:18-19; 2 Samuel 21:3-6; 1 Kings 8:35-36; 1 Kings 21:1-6; 2 Kings 2:9-10; 2 Kings 8:1-6; 2 Chronicles 6:26-27; 2 Chronicles 20:10-11; Ezra 9:10-12; Job 42:15; Psalms 2:7-9;

Psalms 16:5-8; Psalms 16:5-8; Psalms 33:12; Psalms 37:18-19; Psalms 37:21-22; Psalms 37:28-29; Psalms 37:34; Psalms 47:4; Psalms 68:9-10; Psalms 74:2; Psalms 78:55; Psalms 78:62; Psalms 78:71; Psalms 79:1; Psalms 82:8; Psalms 94:3-6; Psalms 94:12-15; Psalms 105:10-11; Psalms 106:4-5; Psalms 106:40-46; Psalms 132:11-18; Psalms 135:8-12; Psalms 136:17-22; Proverbs 11:29; Proverbs 13:22; Proverbs 14:18; Proverbs 11:29; Proverbs 19:14; Proverbs 18:21; Proverbs 28:10; Ecclesiastes 7:11-12; Isaiah 14:21; Isaiah 19:25; Isaiah 47:6-7; Isaiah 49:8; Isaiah 57:13; Isaiah 58:14; Isaiah 61:7; Isaiah 65:9; Jeremiah 2:5-7; Jeremiah 3:18-20; Jeremiah 10:16; Jeremiah 12:7-10; Jeremiah 12:14-17; Jeremiah 16:18; Jeremiah 17:4; Jeremiah 22:22-23; Jeremiah 50:11; Jeremiah 51:19; Lamentations 5:1-3; Ezekiel 11:14; Ezekiel 11:17; Ezekiel 36:12; Ezekiel 44:28; Ezekiel 46:16-18; Ezekiel 47:14; Ezekiel 47:22-23; Joel 2:17; Joel 3:1-3; Micah 7:14; Micah 7:18; Zechariah 2:12; Zechariah 8:12; Malachi 1:2-3; Matthew 5:5; Matthew 21:38; Matthew 25:34-36; Mark 12:1-9; Luke 12:13-15; Luke 14:11-32; Luke 19:9-16; Acts 7:5; Acts 13:17-20; Acts 20:32-35; 1 Corinthians 15:50; Galatians 3:18; Galatians 4:30; Ephesians 1:13-14; Ephesians 5:3-7; Colossians 1:12; Hebrews 6:12; Hebrews 9:15; Hebrews 11:8; 1 Peter 1:3-5; Revelation 21:6-7

Interest

Exodus 22:25; Leviticus 25:36-37; Deuteronomy 23:19-20; Nehemiah 5:3-12; Psalms 15:5; Proverbs 28:8; Ecclesiastes 3:17-23; Ezekiel 18:7-8; Ezekiel 18:12-13; Ezekiel 22:12; Ezekiel 35:15; Ezekiel 45:1-2; Ezekiel 48:29; Daniel 12:13; Obadiah 1:17; Matthew 25:26-28; Luke 19:13-27; Hebrews 12:16-17

Investment

Genesis 47:27; Proverbs 10:4-5; Proverbs 31:16; Ecclesiastes 3:4-9; Ecclesiastes 3:1-8; Ecclesiastes 11:1-2; Ecclesiastes 11:6; Matthew 25:14-30; Luke 19:13-27

Jewelry

Song of Solomon 1:9-11; Song of Solomon 3:9-10; Song of Solomon 4:9; Song of Solomon 5:11-15; Song of Solomon 7:1; Isaiah 3:18-23; Isaiah 13:19; Isaiah 54:11-12; Isaiah 61:10; Jeremiah 2:22; Jeremiah 4:30; Lamentations 4:7-8; Ezekiel 7:20; Ezekiel 10:1; Ezekiel 10:9; Ezekiel 16:11-13; Ezekiel 16:17; Ezekiel 16:39; Ezekiel 21:25-27; Ezekiel 23:26; Ezekiel 23:40; Ezekiel 23:42; Ezekiel 38:13-16; Daniel 11:38;

Hosea 2:13; Hosea 10:1-2; Micah 5:13; Zechariah 9:16; Matthew 7:6; Matthew 13:44-45; Luke 21:5; 1 Timothy 6:10; James 2:1-11; 1 Peter 3:3-4; Revelations 17:4; Revelations 21:11; Revelations 21:15-21

Judgement
Genesis 21:14-18; Psalms 72:3-7; Proverbs 17:26; Matthew 5:25-26

Justice
Exodus 23:2-3; Exodus 23:6; Exodus 23:8; Deuteronomy 16:19-20; Psalms 140:12; Psalms 145:13-16; Isaiah 10:4; Isaiah 11:3-5; Jeremiah 7:5-8; Ezekiel 13:17-18; Ezekiel 13:20; Matthew 17:23-35

Law
Exodus 21:16; Exodus 21:18; Exodus 21:22-25; Exodus 21:28-32; Exodus 21:33-34; Exodus 21:35-36; Exodus 22:1-17; Exodus 22:25-27; Exodus 23:10-11; Ruth 4:3-10

Lazy
Proverbs 6:6-11; Proverbs 10:4-5; Proverbs 10:22; Proverbs 12:27; Proverbs 13:4; Proverbs 15:19; Proverbs 19:14; Proverbs 19:24; Proverbs 20:4; Proverbs 20:13; Proverbs 21:25-26; Proverbs 22:13; Proverbs 23:19-21; Proverbs 24:30-34; Proverbs 26:14-16; Proverbs 28:7; Proverbs 31:27; Ecclesiastes 4:5-6; Ecclesiastes 10:18; Hebrews 6:12

Lender
1 Kings 4:1; Psalms 37:26; Psalms 112:5; Psalms 109:11; Proverbs 6:1-6; Proverbs 19:17; Proverbs 22:7; Proverbs 28:8; Isaiah 24:2-3

Loan
Exodus 22:25-27; Leviticus 25:35-38; Deuteronomy 15:1-11; Deuteronomy 23:19-20; Deuteronomy 24:10-13; Deuteronomy 24:17-18; Deuteronomy 28:12; Deuteronomy 28:44; Nehemiah 5:3-12; Job 24:1-3; Job 24:5-12; Psalms 15:5; Psalms 37:21-22; Proverbs 11:15; Proverbs 17:18; Proverbs 20:16; Proverbs 22:7; Proverbs 22:26-27; Proverbs 27:13; Isaiah 50:1; Jeremiah 15:10; Ezekiel 18:7-8; Ezekiel 18:12-13; Ezekiel 18:16-17; Ezekiel 33:14-15; Amos 2:6-8; Habakkuk 2:6-9; Matthew 5:42; Matthew 6:12; Matthew 18:23-35; Luke 6:34-35; Luke 7:41-44; Luke 11:5-6; Luke 16:1-15; Romans 13:7; Romans 15:27; Philippians 1:18

Loot
Genesis 34:25-29; Exodus 3:22; Exodus 11:2-3; Exodus 12:35-36;

Numbers 31:9-12; Numbers 31:25-27; Deuteronomy 2:35; Deuteronomy 3:7; Deuteronomy 3:12-20; Deuteronomy 4:20-22; Deuteronomy 20:10-18; Joshua 6:19, 24; Joshua 8:2, 27; Joshua 11:13-15; Joshua 22:6-8; Judges 5:19, 30; Judges 8:23-27; 1 Samuel 15:3, 8-9, 15, 20-23; 1 Samuel 23:5; 1 Samuel 27:8-9; 1 Samuel 30:16-26; 2 Samuel 3:22; 2 Samuel 8:7-12; 2 Samuel 12:29-31; 1 Kings 14:25-26; 2 Kings 3:21-23; 2 Kings 7:16; 2 Kings 14:14; 1 Kings 21:14-15; 1 Kings 24:13; 1 Kings 25:13-17; 1 Chronicles 18:7-11; 1 Chronicles 20:1-3; 2 Chronicles 12:9; 2 Chronicles 14:12-14; 2 Chronicles 15:10-11; 2 Chronicles 20:25; 2 Chronicles 24:23; 2 Chronicles 25:13; 2 Chronicles 25:23-24; 2 Chronicles 28:8; 2 Chronicles 28:14-15; 2 Chronicles 36:6-7; 2 Chronicles 36:18; Esther 3:13; Esther 8:1; Esther 9:7-10; Esther 9:15; Psalms 68:11-14; Psalms 105:25-38; Psalms 109:11; Proverbs 1:13-16; Proverbs 16:19; Proverbs 24:15-16; Isaiah 9:2-3; Isaiah 10:6; Isaiah 10:12-14; Isaiah 11:14; Isaiah 13:16; Isaiah 21:2; Isaiah 24:2-3; Isaiah 33:4; Isaiah 33:23; Isaiah 39:4-7; Isaiah 42:18-25; Isaiah 49:24-26; Isaiah 53:12; Jeremiah 2:14; Jeremiah 5:15-17; Jeremiah 15:12-14; Jeremiah 17:3; Jeremiah 20:5; Jeremiah 30:16; Jeremiah 50:10-11; Jeremiah 50:37-38; Jeremiah 52:17-23; Ezekiel 7:21-22; Ezekiel 23:46; Ezekiel 25:6-7; Ezekiel 26:1-6; Ezekiel 26:12; Ezekiel 29:19-20; Ezekiel 34:8-10; Ezekiel 34:22; Ezekiel 34:27-28; Ezekiel 36:4; Ezekiel 38:12-13; Ezekiel 39:10; Daniel 1:2; Daniel 11:8; Daniel 11:24; Daniel 11:33; Daniel 11:43; Hosea 13:15; Amos 3:10-11; Obadiah 1:5-6; Obadiah 1:10; Obadiah 1:13; Nahum 2:9-10; Nahum 3:1; Habakkuk 2:6-9; Zephaniah 2:9; Zechariah 2:7-9; Zechariah 14:1; Zechariah 14:14; Mark 3:27; Luke 11:21-22

Merchant

Ezekiel 27:3; Ezekiel 27:9; Ezekiel 27:12-27; Ezekiel 27:32-33; Zephaniah 1:11; Acts 16:14; Acts 21:3; James 4:13-17; Revelations 18:11-17; Revelations 18:23

Offering

Exodus 22:29-30; Numbers 31:48-54; Joshua 22:26-29; 1 Samuel 9:5-9; 2 Samuel 24:24-25; 2 Kings 12:4-16; 2 Chronicles 24:4-6; 2 Chronicles 29:31; Ezra 7:15-29; Ezra 8:24-34; Nehemiah 7:70-72; Nehemiah 13:8-13; Nehemiah 13:31; Psalms 40:6; Psalms 50:8-15; Psalms 54:6; Psalms 56:12-13; Psalms 116:17-19; Isaiah 1:10-15; Isaiah 19:21; Ezekiel 20:28; Ezekiel 20:31; Ezekiel 20:39-40; Hosea 8:13; Amos 4:4-5; Micah 5:6-8; Malachi 3:8-12; Mark 12:41-44; Luke 5:14; Luke 21:1-4; John 8:20;

Acts 21:26; Acts 24:17; 1 Corinthians 16:1-4; 2 Corinthians 8:19-21; Philippians 4:15-19; Hebrews 10:5-10; Hebrews 11:4

Offering, Specific

Exodus 25:1-9; Exodus 30:11-16; Exodus 32:2-4; Exodus 35:4-9; Exodus 35:20-29; Exodus 37:2-7; Leviticus 5:14-17; Leviticus 6:1-7; Numbers 8:10-88; Numbers 18:14-19; Numbers 29:39; Deuteronomy 12:5-6; Deuteronomy 12:11; Deuteronomy 12:17-19; Deuteronomy 12:26; Deuteronomy 14:22-29; Deuteronomy 16:10; Deuteronomy 16:16-17; Nehemiah 10:32-39; Nehemiah 12:44

Payment

Genesis 31:39; Genesis 31:42; Genesis 37:28; Genesis 42:3-12; Genesis 43:1-26; Genesis 45:4-5; Genesis 47:14-26; Exodus 2:9; Leviticus 25:14-17; 2 Samuel 24:23-24; Job 34:10-15; Psalms 103:8-12; Ezekiel 16:31-34; Ezekiel 16:41; Matthew 27:3-10; Mark 5:26; Luke 10:35; Luke 12:6-7; Luke 14:18-19; John 6:5-7; Acts 1:18-19; Acts 22:28; Acts 24:17; 1 Corinthians 6:19-20; 1 Corinthians 7:23; Philippians 4:15-19; Hebrews 12:16-17; 1 Peter 1:18-19; Revelation 6:6; Revelation 14:4

Planning Ahead

Proverbs 6:5-11; Proverbs 15:22; Proverbs 20:18; Proverbs 20:25; Proverbs 21:5; Proverbs 21:30; Proverbs 24:27; Proverbs 27:1; Proverbs 31:16; Isaiah 5:1-2; Isaiah 28:23-29; Jeremiah 29:4-9; Jeremiah 29:28; Jeremiah 31:4-5; Haggai 2:16-19; Matthew 6:19-21; Matthew 6:25-24; Matthew 10:9-10; Matthew 25:14-30; Mark 6:8-11; Luke 9:3; Luke 10:2-3; Luke 12:16-21; Luke 14:28-30; Luke 19:13-27; Luke 22:35-37; 1 Timothy 5:3-10; James 4:13-17; James 5:1-6

Poor

Job 24:5-12; Job 30:3-8; Job 30:24-26; Job 31:16-23; Job 34:23-30; Psalms 9:18; Psalms 12:5-8; Psalms 14:6; Psalms 15:5; Psalms 22:25-26; Psalms 34:6; Psalms 35:10; Psalms 37:14-15; Psalms 40:17; Psalms 49; Psalms 68:9-10; Psalms 70:5; Psalms 72:3-7; Psalms 72:12-14; Psalms 74:21; Psalms 82:2-4; Psalms 86:1; Psalms 94:3-6; Psalms 109:21-22; Psalms 112:9; Psalms 113:7-9; Psalms 140:12; Psalms 146:6-9; Proverbs 17:5; Proverbs 18:23; Proverbs 19:1; Proverbs 19:4; Proverbs 19:17; Proverbs 20:13; Proverbs 21:5; Proverbs 21:17; Proverbs 22:9; Proverbs 22:16; Proverbs 22:22-23; Proverbs 28:3; Proverbs 28:6; Proverbs 28:27; Proverbs 29:13-14; Proverbs 30:7-9; Ecclesiastes 6:7-9; Ecclesiastes

9:13-18; Isaiah 1:16-17; Isaiah 3:13-15; Isaiah 9:17; Isaiah 10:1-4; Isaiah 11:3-5; Isaiah 25:4; Isaiah 32:5-7; Isaiah 26:5-6; Isaiah 40:19-20; Isaiah 41:17; Isaiah 58:7; Isaiah 58:9-10; Isaiah 61:1; Jeremiah 2:34; Jeremiah 5:4-5; Jeremiah 5:26-29; Jeremiah 20:13; Jeremiah 22:15-17; Jeremiah 39:10; Jeremiah 52:15-16; Ezekiel 16:49; Ezekiel 18:7-8; Ezekiel 18:12-13; Ezekiel 18:16-17; Ezekiel 22:29; Amos 2:6-8; Amos 4:1; Amos 5:11-12; Amos 8:4-6; Zechariah 7:10; Malachi 3:5; Matthew 5:3; Matthew 6:1-4; Matthew 11:5; Matthew 19:18-24; Matthew 26:6-13; Mark 10:18-22; Mark 12:41-44; Mark 14:3-9; Luke 4:18-19; Luke 6:20; Luke 7:22; Luke 11:41; Luke 12:32-34; Luke 14:12-14; Luke 14:21; Luke 18:20-25; Luke 19:2-8; John 12:1-8; John 13:29; Acts 9:36; Acts 10:4; Acts 10:30-31; Acts 24:17; Romans 15:26-28; 1 Corinthians 13:3; 2 Corinthians 6:10; 2 Corinthians 8:1-5; 2 Corinthians 8:9; 2 Corinthians 9:6-15; Galatians 2:10; 1 Timothy 5:3-8; James 2:1-11; Revelations 2:9; Revelations 3:17-18; Revelations 13:16-17

Possessions
Genesis 46:6; Psalms 135:3-4; Ecclesiastes 6:1-6; Ezekiel 33:23-26; Ezekiel 35:10; Ezekiel 36:2-3; Ezekiel 36:5; Ezekiel 44:28; Micah 2:4; Zechariah 9:3-4; Zechariah 4:1; Malachi 3:17; Matthew 12:29; Matthew 18:12-14; Matthew 19:18-24; Matthew 24:45-51; Matthew 25:11; Luke 6:25; Luke 11:21-22; Luke 12:13-15; Luke 12:32-34; Luke 12:42-46; Luke 16:1-15; Luke 17:31-32; Luke 19:2-8; Acts 2:44-45; Acts 4:32-37; 2 Corinthians 12:14; Hebrews 10:34-35; 1 Peter 2:9; 1 John 3:17-18

Poverty
Job 5:5; Proverbs 6:6-11; Proverbs 10:4-5; Proverbs 10:15-16; Proverbs 11:24-26; Proverbs 12:9; Proverbs 13:7-8; Proverbs 13:18; Proverbs 13:23; Proverbs 13:25; Proverbs 17:1; Proverbs 19:7; Proverbs 23:19-21; Proverbs 24:30-34; Proverbs 27:10; Proverbs 28:11; Proverbs 28:22; Ecclesiastes 4:13-16

Profit
Job 34:5-9; Job 35:1-3; Proverbs 21:5; Proverbs 22:7; Proverbs 28:8; Proverbs 29:7; Proverbs 29:13; Proverbs 30:11-14; Proverbs 31:8-9; Ecclesiastes 5:8-20; Ecclesiastes 6:10-11; Isaiah 16:9-10; Ezekiel 18:7-8; Ezekiel 18:12-13; Ezekiel 18:16-17; Ezekiel 22:12-13; Ezekiel 22:27; Judges 1:11; 1 Corinthians 2:17

Property

Leviticus 25:25-28; Leviticus 25:29-34; Ezra 10:8; Psalms 4:6-7; Ecclesiastes 6:1-6

Promise

Leviticus 26:3-45; 2 Chronicles 27:5-6; Psalms 132:11-18

Prosperity

Genesis 30:43; Genesis 32:9; Genesis 32:12; Genesis 39:2; Leviticus 25:26; Leviticus 25:49; Deuteronomy 5:33; Deuteronomy 6:24; Deuteronomy 7:12-15; Deuteronomy 8:6-18; Deuteronomy 28:63; Deuteronomy 29:9; Deuteronomy 30:1-10; Deuteronomy 30:15-17; Joshua 1:8; Judges 18:7; 1 Kings 2:3; 1 Chronicles 29:11-12; 1 Chronicles 29:23; 1 Chronicles 29:26-28; 2 Chronicles 1:11-12; 2 Chronicles 14:7; 2 Chronicles 24:20; 2 Chronicles 27:5-6; 2 Chronicles 31:21; Ezra 6:14; Ezra 6:18; Job 1:1-3; Job 1:9-10; Job 5:24; Job 8:6-7; Job 11:13-19; Job 20:21; Job 21:7-16; Job 22:21-25; Job 36:11; Job 42:10-15; Psalms 1:1-3; Psalms 4:6; Psalms 10:2-9; Psalms 10:14; Psalms 10:17-18; Psalms 22:29-31; Psalms 25:12-15; Psalms 37:10-11; Psalms 37:18-19; Psalms 37:37; Psalms 49; Psalms 51:18; Psalms 66:10; Psalms 72:3-7; Psalms 73:3-11; Psalms 92:12-15; Psalms 106:4-5; Psalms 112:1-5; Psalms 122:6-9; Psalms 128; Psalms 144:13-15; Proverbs 3:2; Proverbs 8:18; Proverbs 11:10-11; Proverbs 11:25; Proverbs 13:25; Proverbs 14:18; Proverbs 15:25; Proverbs 16:20; Proverbs 17:20; Proverbs 19:8; Proverbs 21:21; Proverbs 28:13; Proverbs 28:25; Ecclesiastes 6:1-6; Isaiah 14:30; Isaiah 40:1-2; Isaiah 45:5-7; Isaiah 53:10; Jeremiah 10:21; Jeremiah 12:1; Jeremiah 17:6; Jeremiah 22:30; Jeremiah 29:7; Jeremiah 29:11; Jeremiah 31:23; Jeremiah 32:42; Jeremiah 33:9; Jeremiah 39:16; Jeremiah 40:7; Jeremiah 17:5-8; Jeremiah 22:30; Jeremiah 29:4-14; Jeremiah 31:23; Jeremiah 32:42-44; Jeremiah 33:6-9; Jeremiah 33:11; Jeremiah 39:16; Lamentations 3:16-18; Ezekiel 26:1-6; Ezekiel 36:11; Daniel 4:1; Daniel 4:4; Daniel 4:27; Daniel 6:25; Daniel 6:28; Daniel 8:12; Daniel 8:25; Daniel 10:2; Hosea 10:1-2; Zechariah 1:16-17; Zechariah 7:7; Malachi 3:15; Acts 13:17-20

Ransom

1 Kings 10:39-40; Job 6:22-23; Job 8:2-7; Isaiah 45:13

Redeem

Exodus 6:6; Exodus 13:13-15; Exodus 15:13; Exodus 21:8; Exodus

21:30; Exodus 21:30; Exodus 34:20; Leviticus 25:25-54; Leviticus 27:13-33; Numbers 3:46-49; Numbers 18:15-17; Deuteronomy 7:8; Deuteronomy 9:26; Deuteronomy 13:5; Deuteronomy 15:15; Deuteronomy 21:8; Deuteronomy 24:18; Ruth 2:20; Ruth 3:9-13; Ruth 4:1-14; 2 Samuel 7:23; 1 Chronicles 17:21; Nehemiah 1:10; Job 19:25; Psalms 19:14; Psalms 49:7; Psalms 49:15; Psalms 74:2; Psalms 77:15; Psalms 78:35; Psalms 78:42; Psalms 103:4; Psalms 106:10; Psalms 107:2; Psalms 119:134; Psalms 119:154; Psalms 130:8; Isaiah 29:22; Isaiah 35:1-9; Isaiah 41:14; Isaiah 43:1; Isaiah 43:14; Isaiah 44:6; Isaiah 44:22-24; Isaiah 47:4; Isaiah 48:17-20; Isaiah 49:7; Isaiah 49:26; Isaiah 51:10; Isaiah 52:3-9; Isaiah 54:5-8; Isaiah 59:20; Isaiah 60:16; Isaiah 62:12; Isaiah 63:4-9; Isaiah 63:16; Jeremiah 31:11; Jeremiah 32:8; Jeremiah 50:34; Lamentations 3:58; Hosea 7:13; Hosea 13:14; Micah 4:10; Micah 6:4; Zechariah 10:8; Luke 1:68; Luke 24:21; Galatians 3:13-14; Galatians 4:5; Titus 2:14; 1 Peter 1:18; Revelations 14:3

Refine
Zechariah 13:9; Malachi 3:2-4

Repay
Ezekiel 7:3-4; Ezekiel 7:8-9; Ezekiel 17:19; Romans 11:33-36; Romans 12:17-21; 2 Timothy 4:14; Hebrews 10:30; 1 Peter 3:9; Revelations 17:6-8

Restitution
Numbers 5:5-10; Deuteronomy 28:1-14; Job 42:10-15; Psalms 69:4; Psalms 79:12; Psalms 126:4-6; Jeremiah 30:18; Jeremiah 31:8-9; Jeremiah 31:11-12; Jeremiah 33:6-9; Jeremiah 42:10-12; Jeremiah 48:47; Joel 3:1-8; Micah 6:4; Zephaniah 3:9; Zechariah 1:16-17; Matthew 19:28-30; Mark 10:29-31; Luke 14:12-14; Luke 18:29-30; 1 Timothy 1:12-14; 1 Thessalonians 5:15; 2 Thessalonians 1:6-7

Restore
Deuteronomy 30:3; 2 Samuel 9:7; 2 Samuel 16:12; 2 Chronicles 24:12; 2 Chronicles 33:16; 2 Chronicles 34:10; Ezra 4:13; Nehemiah 3:8; Job 8:6; Job 22:23; Job 33:26; Job 42:10-15; Psalms 69:4; Psalms 71:20; Psalms 85:1; Psalms 126:1; Psalms 126:4; Isaiah 49:8; Jeremiah 30:3; Jeremiah 30:18; Jeremiah 32:44; Jeremiah 33:11; Jeremiah 33:26; Jeremiah 42:12; Jeremiah 48:47; Jeremiah 49:6; Jeremiah 49:39; Ezekiel 16:53; Ezekiel 39:25; Joel 3:1-3; Nahum 2:2; Zephaniah 2:7; Zephaniah 3:20; Zechari-

ah 9:12; Zechariah 10:6

Retirement
Numbers 8:23-26; Proverbs 21:5; Proverbs 21:20; Proverbs 31:23; Zechariah 8:4

Reward
1 Samuel 17:25; 2 Samuel 18:11-13; 1 Chronicles 29:11-12; Job 42:10-15; Psalms 17:13-14; Psalms 18:20-24; Psalms 22:29-31; Psalms 105:42-45; Psalms 112:1-5; Proverbs 13:21; Ecclesiastes 9:5-6; Isaiah 9:2-3; 1 Corinthians 3:12-15; 1 Corinthians 9:17-18; Hebrews 10:34-35; Revelations 11:18; Revelations 22:12-13

Ruin
Deuteronomy 8:19-20; Jeremiah 2:20; Luke 14:11-32

Sabbath
Exodus 16:23-29; Exodus 20:7-11; Exodus 23:10-13; Exodus 31:12-16; Exodus 35:1-3; Leviticus 15:31; Leviticus 19:3; Leviticus 19:30; Leviticus 23:3; Leviticus 23:24; Leviticus 23:32; Leviticus 26:2; Numbers 15:32-36; Deuteronomy 5:12-15; Nehemiah 10:31; Nehemiah 13:15-22; Isaiah 56:2-6; Isaiah 58:13; Jeremiah 17:21-27; Ezekiel 20:12-24; Ezekiel 44:24; Amos 8:5; Matthew 12:3-8; Matthew 12:10-14; Mark 2:23-28; Mark 3:1-4; Luke 6:1-9; Luke 13:10-16; Luke 14:1-5; John 5:9-18; John 7:22-23; John 9:14-16; Colossians 2:16-17; Hebrews 4:8-11

Savings
Job 38:22-23; Luke 14:8-10; 2 Corinthians 12:14

Selling
Genesis 23:4; Genesis 23:9; Genesis 25:31; Genesis 25:33; Genesis 37:27; Genesis 45:5; Genesis 47:16; Genesis 47:22; Exodus 21:7; Exodus 21:8; Exodus 21:35; Exodus 22:1; Leviticus 25:14; Leviticus 25:15; Leviticus 25:25; Leviticus 25:29; Leviticus 25:37; Leviticus 25:39; Leviticus 25:47; Deuteronomy 2:28; Deuteronomy 14:21; Deuteronomy 15:12; Deuteronomy 21:14; Deuteronomy 24:7; Ruth 4:3; 1 Kings 21:6; 1 Kings 21:15; 2 Kings 4:7; 2 Kings 7:1; 2 Kings 7:18; 1 Chronicles 21:22; Nehemiah 5:8; Nehemiah 10:31; Nehemiah 13:15; Nehemiah 13:16; Nehemiah 13:20; Proverbs 11:26; Proverbs 23:23; Proverbs 31:24; Isaiah 24:2; Isaiah 50:1; Ezekiel 7:12; Ezekiel 7:13; Ezekiel 30:12;

Ezekiel 48:14; Joel 3:8; Amos 2:6; Amos 8:5; Amos 8:6; Zechariah 11:5; Matthew 19:21; Matthew 21:12; Matthew 25:9; Mark 10:21; Mark 11:15; Luke 12:33; Luke 17:28; Luke 18:22; Luke 19:45; Luke 22:36; John 2:14; Revelation 13:17

Servant

Deuteronomy 15:12-18; Deuteronomy 24:7; 1 Kings 5:13-18; 1 Kings 9:15-23; 2 Chronicles 8:7-9; Job 41:1-4; Ecclesiastes 3:4-9; Jeremiah 34:14; Matthew 6:24; Colossians 4:1; 1 Timothy 1:8-11; 1 Timothy 6:1-2; Titus 2:9-10; Philippians 1:15-17; 1 Peter 2:18-25; Revelations 6:15; Revelations 19:18

Source

Genesis 14:22-24; Job 5:8-16; Job 22:17-20; Job 22:21-25; Job 16:24-28; Job 36:27-33; Psalms 16:5-8; Psalms 24:1-2; Psalms 34:8-14; Psalms 40:17; Psalms 49; Psalms 65:9-13; Psalms 67:6-7; Psalms 68:5-6; Psalms 68:9-10; Psalms 85:12; Psalms 104:10-18; Psalms 107:33-38; Psalms 142:5-7; Psalms 145:13-16; Psalms 146:6-9; Psalms 147:8-11; Proverbs 3; Proverbs 11:28; Proverbs 22:2; Proverbs 28:26; Ecclesiastes 2:24-26; Isaiah 17:10-11; Isaiah 25:6; Isaiah 30:23-26; Isaiah 45:5-7; Isaiah 48:12-15; Jeremiah 17:5-8; Haggai 2:8; Matthew 6:25-34; Acts 14:14-17; 1 Timothy 6:17-19

Standard

Job 23:10; Psalms 12:5-8; Psalms 100:3; Psalms 102:24-28; Proverbs 16:11; Proverbs 17:3

Tax

Genesis 47:23-26; Judges 3:17-18; Judges 9:3-4; 1 Kings 4:21; 1 Kings 4:27-28; 1 Kings 9:14; 1 Kings 10:14; Ezra 4:13; Nehemiah 5:15-16; Esther 10:1; Isaiah 33:18; Daniel 11:20; Amos 5:11; Matthew 5:46; Matthew 9:9-12; Matthew 10:3; Matthew 11:18-19; Matthew 17:24-27; Matthew 18:17; Matthew 21:31-32; Matthew 22:17-21; Mark 2:14-17; Mark 12:14-17; Luke 3:12-13; Luke 5:27-32; Luke 7:25; Luke 7:33-34; Luke 15:1-2; Luke 18:10-14; Luke 19:2-8; Luke 20:22-25; Luke 23:2; Romans 13:6-7

Theft

Deuteronomy 5:19; Joshua 7:11-12; Joshua 7:20-25; 1 Samuel 12:3-5; Job 24:13-21; Psalms 35:10; Psalms 50:17-18; Psalms 62:10; Proverbs 6:30-31; Proverbs 9:16-18; Proverbs 13:11; Proverbs 19:26; Proverbs

20:10; Proverbs 24:15-16; Proverbs 28:24; Proverbs 30:7-9; Isaiah 1:23; Isaiah 10:1-4; Isaiah 38:10; Jeremiah 21:12; Jeremiah 22:3; Ezekiel 18:7-8; Ezekiel 18:12-13; Ezekiel 18:16-17; Ezekiel 18:18; Ezekiel 22:29; Ezekiel 28:18; Hosea 4:2; Hosea 7:1-2; Habakkuk 2:6-9; Zechariah 5:3; Malachi 3:8-12; Matthew 6:19-21; Matthew 12:29; Matthew 15:16-20; Matthew 19:18-24; Mark 7:20-23; Mark 10:18-22; Mark 11:15-17; Luke 6:30; Luke 10:30-37; Luke 12:39; Luke 18:10-14; Luke 18:20-25; Luke 19:45-46; John 10:1; John 10:8-10; John 12:1-8; Acts 19:37; Romans 2:17-24; Romans 13:8-10; 1 Corinthians 6:9-10; 1 Corinthians 11:7-9; Ephesians 4:28; 1 Thessalonians 5:1-4; Titus 2:9-10; 1 Peter 4:15; 2 Peter 3:10; Revelations 3:3; Revelations 9:21; Revelations 16:15

Tithe

Genesis 14:18-20; Exodus 23:19; Leviticus 27:30-33; Numbers 18:21-19; Deuteronomy 26:1-15; 1 Kings 9:28; 2 Chronicles 24:4-6; 2 Chronicles 24:8-10; 2 Chronicles 31:4-16; Nehemiah 10:32-39; Nehemiah 13:4-5; Malachi 3:8-12; Matthew 23:23; Luke 11:42

Trade

2 Chronicles 1:14-17; Isaiah 23:17-18; Ezekiel 28:4-5

Transaction

Genesis 23; Genesis 33:18-19; Genesis 34:11-12; Exodus 21:2-11; Deuteronomy 2:6; Deuteronomy 2:28-29; Joshua 24:32; 1 Samuel 13:19-21; 2 Samuel 10:6; 1 Kings 5:6-12; 1 Kings 16:24; 1 Kings 21:20-22; 2 Kings 4:7; 1 Chronicles 22:21-26; 2 Chronicles 34:9-11; 2 Chronicles 34:14-17; Ezra 3:7; Ezra 6:8-11; Nehemiah 6:12-13; Nehemiah 13:1-2; Psalms 44:9-12; Psalms 74:2; Proverbs 7:20; Proverbs 23:22-25; Isaiah 24:2-3; Isaiah 52:3; Isaiah 55:1-2; Jeremiah 2:11; Jeremiah 32:6-15; Jeremiah 32:25; Jeremiah 32:42-44; Jeremiah 34:14; Lamentations 5:4; Ezekiel 7:12-13; Ezekiel 48:14; Daniel 11:39; Hosea 3:2; Hosea 8:9-10; Hosea 9:1; Hosea 12:12; Joel 3:4-8; Amos 1:6; Amos 1:9; Amos 2:6-8; Amos 8:4-6; Jonah 1:3; Zephaniah 1:18; Zechariah 11:4-6; Matthew 10:29-31; Matthew 13:44-45; Matthew 14:15; Matthew 21:12-13; Matthew 25:9-10; Matthew 26:6-13; Matthew 26:14-16; Mark 6:35-37; Mark 11:15-17; Mark 14:10-11; Mark 16:1; Luke 17:28-29; Luke 19:45-46; Luke 22:4-6; Luke 22:35-37; John 2:14-17; John 4:7-8; John 12:1-8; John 13:29; Acts 4:33-37; Acts 5:1-11; Acts 7:9-10; Acts 7:16; Romans 7:14; 1 Corinthians 7:29-31; 1 Corinthians 10:25-26; Revelations 3:17-18; Revelations 13:16-17

Treasure
Job 3:20-22; Job 23:12; Job 28:1-11; Proverbs 15:6; Proverbs 24:3-4; Isaiah 2:7-9; Isaiah 33:5-6; Isaiah 39:4-7; Isaiah 45:3; Jeremiah 15:12-14; Lamentations 1:7; Lamentations 1:10-11; Ezekiel 7:21-22; Ezekiel 22:25; Hosea 9:6; Joel 3:4-8; Matthew 6:19-21; Matthew 13:44-45; Matthew 13:52; Matthew 19:18-24; Luke 2:19; Luke 2:51; Luke 12:32-34; Luke 18:20-25; Acts 8:18; Colossians 2:2-3; Hebrews 11:24-26

Treaty
Genesis 22:25-31; Genesis 32:13-16; Genesis 33:10-11; 2 Samuel 8:7-12; 1 Kings 15:18-19; 1 Kings 17:3-4; 1 Chronicles 19:6-7; 2 Chronicles 16:2-3; 2 Chronicles 28:19-21

Tribute
1 Kings 10:1-9; 2 Kings 3:4-5; 2 Kings 12:17-18; 2 Kings 15:19-20; 1 Kings 18:13-16; 1 Kings 23:33-35; 2 Chronicles 8:18; 2 Chronicles 9:13-14; 2 Chronicles 3:11; 2 Chronicles 27:5-6; 2 Chronicles 36:2-3; Ezra 4:13; Isaiah 16:1; Isaiah 30:6-7; Hosea 10:6

Unsatisfying
1 Samuel 2:5; Psalms 127:1-2; Luke 14:11-32; James 5:1-6

Use
1 Chronicles 28:14-18; 2 Chronicles 3:3-17; 2 Chronicles 4:1-2; 2 Chronicles 6:12-13; 2 Chronicles 7:7; 2 Chronicles 9:15-28; 2 Chronicles 12:10-11; 2 Chronicles 24:14; 2 Chronicles 28:24-25; Esther 1:6-7; Esther 4:11; Esther 5:2; Esther 8:4; Job 28:1-11; Psalms 135:15-18; Proverbs 25:4; Song of Solomon 8:8-9; Luke 12:42-46; Luke 16:1-15; Luke 20:9-16; 1 Corinthians 3:12-15; Hebrews 9:1-5

Value
Exodus 19: 3-6; Psalms 19:9-10; Psalms 66:10; Psalms 119:72; Psalms 119:126-128; Proverbs 2:1-5; Proverbs 10:20; Proverbs 11:22; Proverbs 27:21; Ecclesiastes 7:11-12; Ecclesiastes 10:19; Song of Solomon 8:11-12; Isaiah 1:22; Isaiah 7:23; Isaiah 13:11-12; Isaiah 13:17; Isaiah 48:10; Jeremiah 6:27-30; Jeremiah 51:7; Lamentations 4:1-2; Ezekiel 7:19; Ezekiel 9:2; Ezekiel 22:17-22; Ezekiel 27:6-7; Daniel 2:31-45; Daniel 4:15; Daniel 4:23; Daniel 5:2-3; Daniel 7:7; Daniel 7:19; Daniel 10:5-6; Daniel 11:38; Hosea 2:8-9; Micah 4:13; Zechariah 4:1-2; Zechariah 2:12; Matthew 26:6-13; John 12:1-8; Acts 19:19; 2 Timothy 2:20-211;

Peter 1:7; Revelations 1:13-15; Revelations 1:20; Revelations 2:1; Revelations 2:18; Revelations 2:26-27; Revelations 4:3-4; Revelations 5:8; Revelations 8:3; Revelations 9:7-9; Revelations 9:13; Revelations 12:5; Revelations 14:14; Revelations 15:6-7; Revelations 17:4; Revelations 19:15; Revelations 21:15-21

Vows
Deuteronomy 23:21-23; Acts 21:24

Wages
Genesis 29:15; Genesis 30:27-29; Genesis 30:32; Genesis 30:33; Genesis 31:6-8; Genesis 31:41; Leviticus 19:13; Numbers 18:31; Deuteronomy 24:15; 1 Kings 5:6; Proverbs 10:16; Proverbs 11:18; Proverbs 22:4; Hosea 9:1; Micah 1:7; Haggai 1:6; Zechariah 8:10; Malachi 3:5; Matthew 20:8; Mark 6:37; Mark 14:5; Luke 10:7; John 6:7; John 12:5; Romans 4:4; Romans 6:23; 1 Timothy 5:18; James 5:4; 2 Peter 2:15; Revelations 6:6

Wealth
Genesis 13: 1-2; Genesis: 13:6; Genesis 25:34-35; Genesis 27:12-14; 2 Samuel 19:32; 1 Kings 10:14-29; 1 Kings 22:39-40; 1 Kings 20:12-18; 1 Chronicles 22:14-16; 1 Chronicles 29:1-9; 1 Chronicles 29:11-12; 1 Chronicles 29:26-28; 2 Chronicles 9:15-28; 2 Chronicles 17:12-13; 2 Chronicles 18:1-2; 2 Chronicles 30:3; 2 Chronicles 32:27-29; 2 Chronicles 35:7-9; Nehemiah 5:17-18; Esther 1:4; Esther 1:6-7; Esther 5:11; Esther 7:1-2; Job 1:1-3; Job 3:13-15; Job 38:22-23; Psalms 22:29-31; Psalms 37:16-17; Psalms 39:6; Psalms 39:11; Psalms 45:8-9; Psalms 45:10-15; Psalms 62:10; Psalms 49; Psalms 68:11-14; Psalms 73:3-12; Psalms 112:1-5; Proverbs 10:4-5; Proverbs 10:15-16; Proverbs 11:16; Proverbs 12:9; Proverbs 13:7-8; Proverbs 14:18; Proverbs 14:24; Proverbs 18:11; Proverbs 18:23; Proverbs 19:4; Proverbs 21:20; Proverbs 22:7; Proverbs 27:23-27; Proverbs 28:6; Proverbs 28:11; Proverbs 30:8; Ecclesiastes 3:4-9; Ecclesiastes 2:24-26; Ecclesiastes 4:8; Ecclesiastes 5:8-20; Ecclesiastes 6:1-6; Ecclesiastes 6:7-9; Ecclesiastes 9:11-12; Ecclesiastes 10:5-7; Ecclesiastes 10:20; Isaiah 5:16-17; Isaiah 10:1-4; Isaiah 10:12-14; Isaiah 15:7; Isaiah 39:1-2; Isaiah 53:9; Isaiah 60:5-17; Isaiah 61:6; Isaiah 66:12-13; Jeremiah 5:26-29; Jeremiah 9:23-24; Jeremiah 15:12-14; Jeremiah 17:11; Jeremiah 48:7; Jeremiah 48:33; Jeremiah 51:10; Ezekiel 7:11; Ezekiel 7:21-22; Ezekiel 16:53-54; Ezekiel 26:12; Ezekiel 27:27; Ezekiel 27:32-33; Ezekiel 28:4-5; Ezekiel 29:19-20; Eze-

kiel 30:4; Ezekiel 38:12-13; Daniel 11:2; Daniel 11:24; Daniel 11:28; Hosea 12:7-8; Micah 4:13; Micah 6:10-15; Habakkuk 2:6-9; Zephaniah 1:12-13; Zechariah 9:3-4; Matthew 19:18-24; Matthew 25:14-30; Matthew 27:57-61; Mark 10:18-22; Mark 10:23-27; Mark 12:41-44; Luke 1:53; Luke 6:24-25; Luke 8:14; Luke 12:16-21; Luke 14:12-14; Luke 14:11-32; Luke 16:1-15; Luke 16:19-31; Luke 18:20-25; Luke 21:1-4; Romans 2:4; Romans 11:12; Romans 11:33-36; 1 Corinthians 4:8; 2 Corinthians 6:10; 2 Corinthians 8:9; Ephesians 1:7-10; Ephesians 1:18-19; Ephesians 2:4-7; Ephesians 3:8; Ephesians 3:14-19; Colossians 2:2-3; 1 Timothy 6:2-10; 1 Timothy 6:17-19; James 1:9-11; James 2:1-11; James 5:1-6; Revelations 3:17-18; Revelations 5:12; Revelations 6:15; Revelations 13:16-17; Revelations 18:3; Revelations 18:11-19

Wisdom

Job 28:12-19; Job 16:24-28; Job 42:10-15; Proverbs 2:1-5; Proverbs 8:10-11; Proverbs 8:18-21; Proverbs 10:14; Proverbs 11:4; Proverbs 11:24-26; Proverbs 12:15; Proverbs 13:13; Proverbs 14:4; Proverbs 15:17; Proverbs 16:16; Proverbs 17:16; Proverbs 19:3; Proverbs 19:8; Proverbs 20:15; Proverbs 22:1; Proverbs 22:4; Proverbs 22:16; Proverbs 23:4-5; Proverbs 23:22-25; Proverbs 24:3-4; Proverbs 24:27; Proverbs 25:11-12; Proverbs 26:23; Proverbs 28:11; Proverbs 28:20; Proverbs 28:22; Proverbs 29:3; Proverbs 30:7-9; Ecclesiastes 4:13-16; Ecclesiastes 6:7-9; Ecclesiastes 7:11-12; Ecclesiastes 9:13-18; Ecclesiastes 10:5-7; Isaiah 1:16-17; Colossians 2:2-3

Women

Deuteronomy 21:10-14; Deuteronomy 2:13-19; Deuteronomy 22:28-29; Psalms 68:11-14; Psalms 113:7-9; Psalms 146:6-9; Proverbs 6:26; Proverbs 11:16; Proverbs 11:22; Proverbs 12:4; Proverbs 14:1; Proverbs 31; Isaiah 10:1-4; Isaiah 32:9-15; Isaiah 50:1; Jeremiah 7:5-8; Jeremiah 22:3; Jeremiah 31:8-9; Ezekiel 22:6; Ezekiel 22:25; Hosea 12:12; Mark 12:40; Acts 16:14

Work

Proverbs 10:4-5; 2 Thessalonians 3:7-15; Revelations 14:13

Workers

Leviticus 25:39-46; Leviticus 25:47-55; Deuteronomy 24:14-15; 1 Kings 22:4-9; 2 Chronicles 24:12; 2 Chronicles 25:6-9; Job 7:1-3; Job 31:13-15; Job 31:38-40; Proverbs 6:6-11; Ecclesiastes 3:10-11; Ecclesiastes

3:17-23; Ecclesiastes 3:9-14; Ecclesiastes 3:22; Ecclesiastes 4:4; Ecclesiastes 4:8; Ecclesiastes 4:9-12; Ecclesiastes 5:8-20; Ecclesiastes 6:7-9; Ecclesiastes 8:15; Revelations 18:22

CPSIA information can be obtained
at www.ICGtesting.com
Printed in the USA
FSHW010946271019
63435FS

9 781640 884755